LAB MANUAL

Second Edition

MOSAICOS

Spanish as a World Language

Matilde O. Castells

Emerita, California State University, Los Angeles

Prentice Hall, Upper Saddle River, New Jersey 07458

Simon & Schuster/A Viacom Company
Upper Saddle River, New Jersey 07458

Printed in the United States of America
10 9 8 7 6 5 4 3 2

ISBN: 0-13-915885-5

Prentice Hall International (UK) Limited, *London*
Prentice Hall of Australia Pty. Limited, *Sydney*
Prentice Hall Canada Inc., *Toronto*
Prentice Hall Hispanoamericana, S.A., *México*
Prentice Hall of India Private Limited, *New Delhi*
Prentice Hall of Japan, Inc. *Tokyo*
Prentice Hall of Southeast Asia Pte. Ltd, *Singapore*
Editora Prentice Hall do Brasil, Ltda., *Rio de Janeiro*

Contents

To the instructor

This ***Lab Manual*** is designed to accompany ***Mosaicos: Spanish as a World Language, Second Edition.*** The audio recordings used with the ***Lab Manual*** correspond fully to the presentation of vocabulary and structures in the student textbook, and are focused to enhance students' listening comprehension and speaking. These recordings help familiarize students with Spanish as it is used by native speakers in numerous real-life situations and give them more opportunities to interact with spoken Spanish in meaningful ways outside of class.

Each *lección* in the ***Lab Manual*** is divided into the same sections as the corresponding *lección* in the text: *A primera vista*, *Explicación y expansión*, and *Mosaicos*. In addition, there is a pronunciation section in the *Bienvenidos* chapter, as well as in the first seven *lecciones*. The pronunciation sections focus on the letter/sound correspondence and provide an explanation of the sound followed by examples for students to repeat aloud. Beginning with *lección 2*, stress is included in the pronunciation sections.

The first activities in *lecciones 1* through *15* correspond to the *A primera vista* section of each *lección*. The listening segments for these activities are dialogs, descriptions, announcements, etc. that revolve around the theme found in the corresponding *lección*, followed by true-false or multiple-choice questions, and then by questions that require the students to fill in a chart or write in an answer. In some *lecciones* there are questions that ask students to respond orally or write about their personal experiences.

The next section of laboratory activities corresponds to the *Explicación y expansión* section in the text. This section normally begins with dialogs or descriptions in which the chapter's grammatical structures are presented in functional contexts reflecting real-life situations. These listening comprehension activities are followed by activities which provide students with an opportunity to practice orally what is presented in the section. The oral activities with predictable answers have a confirmation on the tape for students to compare to their own answers.

The listening comprehension activities in the final section, *Mosaicos*, combine the material presented in the *lección* and offer additional opportunities for students to improve their listening skills.

The answers to activities that do not have a confirmation on tape are given in an answer section at the back of the ***Lab Manual.***

The gradual sequencing of listening and speaking in this Lab program will help students build their skills and confidence in Spanish, so that in class they can communicate more effectively with their classmates and instructor and begin to use Spanish creatively to accomplish real-world purposes of their own.

To the student

This ***Lab Manual*** will help you study on your own to improve your listening skills and become a fluent speaker of Spanish. The ***Lab Manual*** listening segments and activities correspond to the vocabulary and grammar that is presented in ***Mosaicos: Spanish as a World Language, Second Edition***. The recordings that accompany the manual will give you ample opportunities outside of class to listen to Spanish as it is used by native speakers in a variety of real-life situations and to practice your spoken Spanish.

Each lesson in the ***Lab Manual*** is divided into the same three sections as the corresponding lesson in your text: *A primera vista*, *Explicación y expansión*, and *Mosaicos*. In addition, the *Bienvenidos* chapter and the first seven lessons contain a pronunciation section.

Each ***Lab Manual*** lesson features listening comprehension segments consisting of conversations, descriptions, announcements, reports, etc. that revolve around the theme of your book's lesson. In order to test your comprehension, these segments are followed by true-false or multiple-choice questions, charts that you fill in, statements that you complete, or questions that you answer. To accomplish these tasks, you do not have to understand every word you hear. Even in your own language, there are many instances in which you do not understand every single word; nevertheless you can follow and comprehend what is been said.

The following suggestions will facilitate your understanding of the recorded passages:

1. Read and/or listen to the title and the instructions carefully to get a general idea of the content of the recording.

2. Pause for a moment and think about the topic and try to anticipate what you may hear. Then, listen to the recording once or go directly to the next step.

3. Read the questions, sentences, charts, etc., to familiarize yourself with the task you will complete.

4. Listen to the recording and focus your attention on the answers to the questions.

5. Listen to the segment as many times as necessary to complete the task.

6. Listen to the tapes on different occasions (while driving or doing chores at home), even after you have completed the tasks. You will notice that this exposure to spoken Spanish will help you increase your comprehension.

The *Explicación y expansión* section contains both listening comprehension passages and contextualized activities that will give you ample opportunities to practice orally what is presented in each lesson. Oral activities with predictable answers have a confirmation so you can compare your answers with those on the tape. An answer section at the back of the ***Lab Manual*** provides the answers to the activities that do not have a confirmation on tape. These answers allow you to check your work and your progress in the course.

The pronunciation sections focus on the letter/sound relationship in Spanish and provide an explanation of the Spanish sounds, followed by examples for you to repeat aloud. Beginning with lesson 2, stress and accentuation are included in the pronunciation sections. The exercises in these sections will help you attune your ear to the differences between Spanish and your native language and improve your pronunciation.

The oral work in the ***Lab Manual*** that you do outside of class will help build your skills and confidence when you speak Spanish. If you do your work thoroughly, either on a daily basis or several times a week, you will notice improvement in your comprehension of spoken Spanish and your speaking ability. As a result, you will be able to communicate more effectively with your classmates and instructor and begin to use Spanish creatively to accomplish real-world purposes.

Lección preliminar
Bienvenidos

Las presentaciones

B-1 Presentaciones. First, listen to the conversations and put an **X** in the appropriate column to indicate if the speakers are addressing each other formally or informally. Then, listen to the conversations again and mark which two expressions in the chart you hear in each conversation. (Do not select any item more than twice.)

	FORMAL	*INFORMAL*
1.	______________	______________
2.	______________	______________
3.	______________	______________

Conversación	1	2	3
mucho gusto			
me llamo Carmen			
encantada			
igualmente			
encantado			

B-2 Mucho gusto. You are meeting two classmates for the first time. Respond to each appropriately in the pauses provided.

1. ______________

   ____

2. ______________

   ____

Saludos, despedidas, expresiones de cortesía

B-3 Saludos. Listen as several people greet each other. First repeat each greeting, then indicate with a check mark in the chart the approximate time it took place.

	1	2	3	4	5
6:00 a.m. - 11:30 a.m.					
1:00 p.m. - 7:00 p.m.					
7:00 p.m. - 2:00 a.m.					

B-4 ¿Tú o usted? Listen to the conversations and then put an **X** in the appropriate column to indicate whether the speakers are addressing each other formally (**usted**) or informally (**tú**).

Conversación	1	2	3
Tú			
Usted			
Tú / Usted			

B-5 ¿Bien, regular o mal? Listen to two short conversations that take place in the bus station. Then put an **X** in the appropriate column to indicate how each speaker is feeling.

Conversación 1	Bien	Regular	Mal
Sra. Gómez			
Sr. Mena			
Conversación 2	**Bien**	**Regular**	**Mal**
Felipe			
Ana			

Nombre: ______________________ Fecha: ______________________

B-6 Cortesía. You will hear several expressions in Spanish. Look at the drawings and write the number corresponding to the appropriate statement.

_____ _____ _____ _____

B-7 Más expresiones. You are planning a trip to Mexico and you want to learn expressions for saying goodbye as well as some polite expressions. Listen and repeat each expression, and then write it next to the appropriate situation below.

1. You say goodbye to someone you will see tomorrow.

   ____

2. You are saying goodbye to someone and you do not know when you will meet again.

   ____

3. You want to request a favor.

   ____

4. You want to thank someone for a favor.

   ____

5. You say goodbye to someone you will meet later today.

   ____

Identificación y descripción de personas

B-8 ¿Sí o no? Listen to two friends talking in the campus lounge and to the statements following their conversation. Indicate whether each statement is true or false by marking **sí** or **no.**

	Sí	*No*
1.	_____	_____
2.	_____	_____
3.	_____	_____
4.	_____	_____

B-9 ¿Cómo son? Professor Sánchez is describing some students. Listen and fill in each blank with the correct word.

1. Felipe Torres es activo y _______________.
2. Ana Ortiz es _______________ y _______________.
3. Martín Gutiérrez es _______________ y sentimental.
4. Pepe Chávez es _______________ y _______________.
5. Alicia Sarmiento es _______________ y _______________.

B-10 Dictado. Listen carefully to a brief comparison of two friends. The first time, just listen. The second time, write the missing words in the blanks. There will be pauses to give you time to write the words.

_______________ Carmen Montes. Yo soy _______________ y _______________.

_______________ Mónica es diferente. Ella es introvertida y _______________.

B-11 El mundo hispano. The speaker will spell the names of several important cities in the Spanish-speaking world. Write them in the spaces provided.

1. ____ ____ ____ ____
2. ____ ____ ____ ____ ____ ____ ____ ____
3. ____ ____ ____ ____ ____ ____
4. ____ ____ ____ ____ ____ ____
5. ____ ____ ____ ____ ____ ____ ____
6. ____ ____ ____ ____ ____ ____ ____

Nombre: ______________________ Fecha: ______________________

Pronunciación

Las vocales

Listen carefully to the explanation of how the Spanish vowels are pronounced. Repeat each of the words after the speaker when asked to do so.

Spanish has five simple vowel sounds, represented in writing by the letters **a, e, i, o,** and **u.** These vowels are tense and short, and, for all practical purposes, constant in length. In order to avoid the glide sound of English stressed vowels (as in *no*, or *same*), do not move your tongue, lips, and jaw. Also, avoid the *uh* sound of English unstressed vowels (as in *opera* and *about*).

a

The pronunciation of the Spanish **a** is similar to the English *a* in *father*, but shorter and tenser. Listen carefully and then repeat. Imitate the Spanish pronunciation as closely as possible.

llama mañana banana Panamá encantada

e

The pronunciation of the Spanish **e** is similar to the English *e* in *they*, but without the glide sound. **Repitan las siguientes palabras.** *(Repeat the following words.)*

sé nene este Sánchez bastante

i

The pronunciation of the Spanish **i** is similar to the pronunciation of the English *i* in *machine*, but without the glide sound. **Repitan las siguientes palabras.**

sí ni Mimí Inés Felipe

o

The pronunciation of the Spanish **o** is similar to the English *o* in *no*, but without the glide sound. **Repitan las siguientes palabras.**

no con Mónica noches profesor

u

The pronunciation of the Spanish **u** is similar to the English *u* in *tuna*, but without the glide sound. **Repitan las siguientes palabras.**

su tú mucho uno usted

¿Qué hay en el salón de clase?

B-12 Identificación. It's the first day of class and you are trying to identify objects and persons around you. Listen to the tape, look for the object or person in the picture, and write the number corresponding to each one in the space provided.

MODELO: 0. *una pizarra*

¿Dónde está?

B-13 ¿Qué es esto? Listen to the question for each of the pictures in your workbook. Answer by identifying the object.

MODELO: 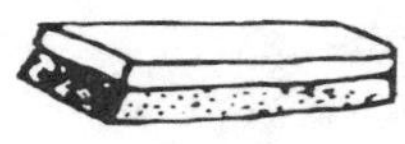 ¿Qué es esto?

Es un borrador.

1. ...

2. ...

3. ...

4. ...

5. ...

6. ...

Nombre: ______________________ Fecha: ______________________

B-14 ¿Qué está. . .? Your instructor is asking questions about the location of several people and objects. Look at the drawing and answer each question.

MODELO: ¿Qué está al lado de la pizarra?
La puerta.

B-15 ¿Dónde está? Look at the drawing again. Your instructor is asking you to locate persons and objects in the room. Answer each question as specifically as possible. Your answer may vary from the one provided as long as your response gives the correct location.

MODELO: ¿Dónde está la pizarra?
Está detrás de la profesora. (*Está al lado de la puerta* would also be correct.)

Los números 0–99

B-16 Los números. Repeat the numbers after the speaker.

B-17 Bingo. Your Spanish Club is playing bingo. Circle each number you hear on the card below.

B	I	N	G	O
B5	I16	N31	G48	O62
B8	I18	N38	G50	O65
B1O	I21		G55	O68
B13	I22	N42	G56	O70
B15	I30	N45	G60	O75

B-18 Problemas de matemáticas. You are helping your little cousin practice addition. Listen to each math problem, write the problem and the correct answer, then repeat the problem, according to the model.

MODELO: You see: _____ + _____ =
You hear: Dos más dos
You write: 2 + 2 = 4
You say: *Dos más dos son cuatro.*

1. _____ + _____ = _____
2. _____ + _____ = _____
3. _____ + _____ = _____
4. _____ + _____ = _____
5. _____ + _____ = _____
6. _____ + _____ = _____
7. _____ + _____ = _____
8. _____ + _____ = _____
9. _____ + _____ = _____

B-19 Urgente. You are a telephone information operator and receive the following requests for phone numbers. Answer each call by giving the correct number.

MODELO: ¡Aló! Por favor, el teléfono de los bomberos. *(firemen)*
bomberos 2-55-11-00
dos, cincuenta y cinco, once, cero, cero

1. aeropuerto 2-31-60-80
2. hospital general 4-75-67-59
3. operadora internacional 51-88
4. la policía 4-82-70-90

Los días de la semana y los meses del año

B-20 Las preguntas de Lupe. Listen and repeat the following conversation. Then complete the information in the chart.

Preguntas	Respuestas
¿Cuántos días hay en una semana?	
	Hay veinticuatro
¿Cuántos días hay en un mes?	

Nombre: ______________________ Fecha: ______________________

B-21 ¿Qué día es? Look at the calendar. You will hear questions asking on what days of the week certain dates fall. Answer each question by naming the appropriate day.

MODELO: ¿Qué día es el 15?
Es jueves

OCTUBRE						
L	**M**	**M**	**J**	**V**	**S**	**D**
			1	2	3	4
5	6	7	8	9	10	11
12	13	14	15	16	17	18
19	20	21	22	23	24	25
26	27	28	29	30	31	

La hora

B-22 ¿Qué hora es? You will hear a time for each watch in your workbook. If the time you hear corresponds to the time shown on the watch, write **sí**. If it doesn't correspond, write **no**.

1. ______ 2. ______ 3. ______ 4. ______ 5. ______

B-23 La hora del tren. You will hear an employee of the train station announcing the arrival times of trains from several cities in Spain. Draw in the hands corresponding to each arrival time on the clock faces. Don't worry if you don't understand every word.

MODELO: El tren de Madrid llega a las once y media.

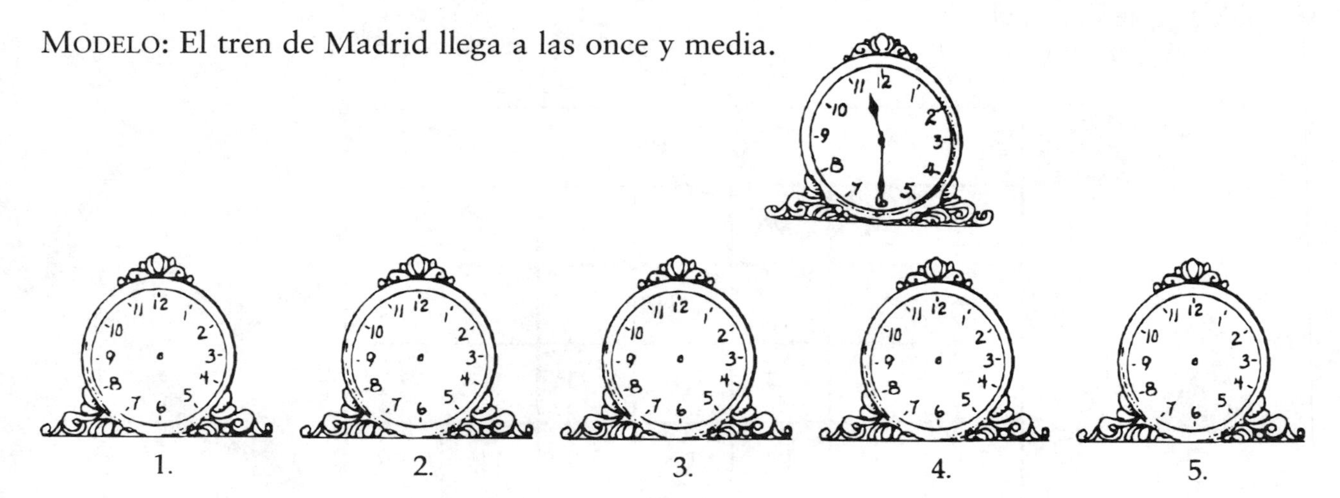

B-24 ¿A qué hora es la clase? Look at the class schedule below and answer each question by saying at what time each class meets.

Modelo: ¿A qué hora es la clase de matemáticas?
A las ocho.

Clase	Hora
matemáticas	8:00
física	9:30
economía	10:15
álgebra	11:20
cálculo	1:00
sociología	2:45

Nombre: ______________________ Fecha: ______________________

Expresiones útiles en la clase

B-25 En la clase. You will hear several useful expressions that are frequently said in class. Write the number corresponding to the expression that describes each drawing in the space provided.

___

___

___

___

Pronunciación

Las consonantes p, t, c, q, s, and z

Listen carefully to the explanation of how some of the Spanish consonants are pronounced. In this section you will learn to pronounce some of the Spanish consonants that are slightly different from their English counterparts. Repeat after the speaker when asked to do so.

p

The Spanish **p** is pronounced like the English *p*, but it is never accompanied by the puff of air that often follows the English *p*. Listen to the pronunciation of these two words and note the differences.

Spanish	*English*
papá	*papa*

Repitan las siguientes palabras.

Pepe pino pan peso poco popular

t

The Spanish **t** is pronounced by placing the tip of the tongue against the back of the upper teeth and is never accompanied by a puff of air. The English *t*, in contrast, is pronounced by placing the tip of the tongue against the ridge of the upper gum, and is often followed by a puff of air. **Repitan las siguientes palabras.**

te tú tomate tres está optimista

c, q, s, and z

The Spanish **c** before a consonant or **a, o,** or **u** is pronounced like an English *k,* but without the puff of air. The Spanish combination of the letters **qu** before **e** or **i** is pronounced like an English *k,* also without a puff of air. **Repitan las siguientes palabras.**

como café cuna típico qué quién

Spanish **c** before **e** or **i** is pronounced like English *c* before *e* or *i.* **Repitan las siguientes palabras.**

cena cita cesto once gracias cinco

s and z

Spanish **s** and **z** are pronounced like the English *s* in *some.* Because of the influence of English, you may tend to pronounce the Spanish **s** as **z** when it occurs between vowels. This is never done in Spanish. **Repitan las siguientes palabras.**

señora está ese casa zeta tiza

Lección 1

Los estudiantes y la universidad

A PRIMERA VISTA

1-1 Mi amigo Juan. You will hear a young man talk about a friend. Complete the statements by marking the appropriate answer according to the information you hear. You may go over the statements before listening to the tape.

1. Juan trabaja por la
   a) mañana. b) tarde. c) noche.
2. Él trabaja en
   a) el laboratorio. b) una oficina. c) la universidad.
3. Su clase favorita es
   a) antropología. b) historia. c) economía.
4. El profesor de historia es
   a) aburrido. b) muy bueno. c) muy activo.

1-2 Dos conversaciones. You will hear two brief conversations. Indicate whether each statement is true or false. Don't worry if there are some words you don't understand.

Sí *No* *Conversación 1*

_____ _____ 1. Ana estudia informática y español.
_____ _____ 2. Ella estudia mucho.
_____ _____ 3. Ana saca muy buenas notas.

Conversación 2

_____ _____ 1. Felipe está muy bien.
_____ _____ 2. Felipe estudia física.
_____ _____ 3. La clase es muy difícil.
_____ _____ 4. Felipe saca muy buenas notas.

1-3 Mario, Carolina y Jim. You have just met these students in the cafeteria. As they tell you about themselves, complete the chart with the information you hear.

Nombre	Clase	¿Cómo es la clase?	¿A qué hora llega?	¿Dónde estudia?
0. *Mario*	*química*	*fácil*	*a las nueve*	*en la biblioteca*
1.	alemán			
2.				

1-4 Las actividades de Perla. You will hear a description of Perla's studies and activities on Mondays. As you listen, complete the chart with the information you hear. Don't worry if you don't understand every word.

Horario	Lugar	Actividades
Por la mañana		
Por la tarde		
Por la noche		

1-5 Preguntas personales. You will hear four questions. Answer them in the pauses provided on the tape.

EXPLICACIÓN Y EXPANSIÓN

Subject pronouns

1-6 ¿Informal o formal? You will hear four persons to whom you have to speak. Put an **X** in the appropriate column to indicate which subject pronoun you would use when addressing each one.

	Tú	*Usted*	*Ustedes*
1.	_____	_____	_____
2.	_____	_____	_____
3.	_____	_____	_____
4.	_____	_____	_____

Nombre: ______________________________ Fecha: ______________________________

1-7 Pronombres personales. Your instructor is talking to the class. Repeat her statements and mark the subject pronouns she is using.

Pronombres	1	2	3	4	5	6
yo						
tú						
Ud.						
él						
ella						
nosotros						
vosotros						
ellos						

Present tense of regular *-ar* verbs

1-8 ¿A qué hora llegan? The chart below shows the times when various students arrive at the Facultad de Medicina. Say that they arrive at the time shown.

MODELO: You see: Linda 8:00 a.m.
You say: *Linda llega a las ocho de la mañana.*

	a.m.	
1.	yo	10:00
2.	Paco	9:00
3.	Juan y Alicia	11:00
	p.m.	
4.	Pepe y yo	2:30
5.	tú	3:00

1-9 No, no. . . Give a negative answer to each question.

MODELO: ¿Hablan ustedes ruso?
No, no hablamos ruso.

Articles and nouns: gender and number

1-10 El plural. Listen to these phrases. Then repeat each one giving the plural form of the noun you hear.

MODELO: Compro el libro.
Compro los libros.

Present tense of the verb *estar*

1-11 ¿Dónde están? Look at the campus map and label the unidentified buildings according to the information you hear.

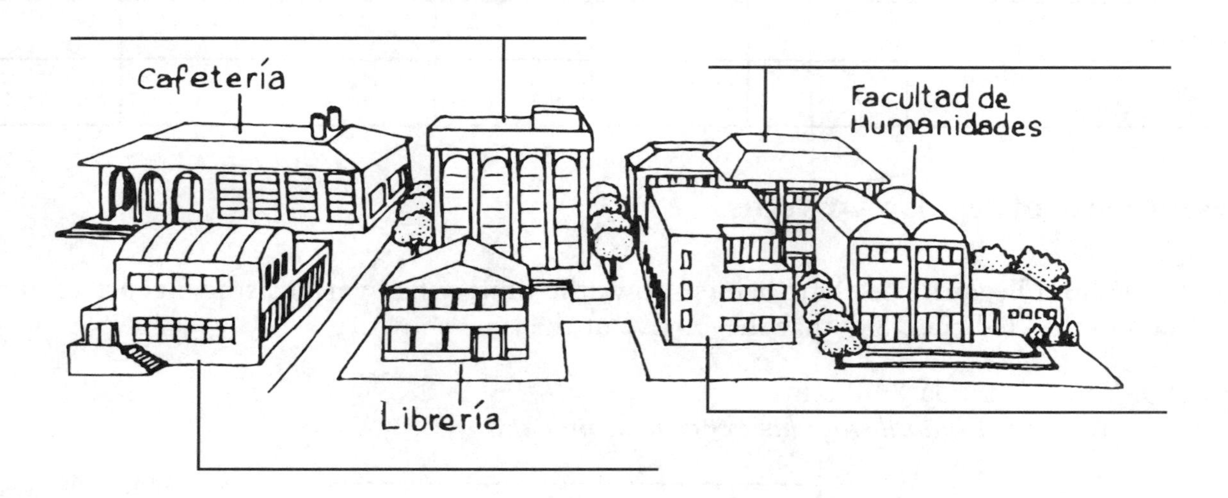

1-12 ¿Dónde? ¿A qué hora? You are telling the basketball coach where to find you and your friends. Using the chart below, say where each of you is at each indicated time.

MODELO: You see: Juan y María laboratorio 3:00
You say: *Juan y María están en el laboratorio a las tres.*

1. usted	gimnasio	8:00
2. Rosa	biblioteca	10:30
3. nosotros	Facultad	11:00
4. ellos	cafetería	1:00
5. Ana y él	clase de física	2:15
6. yo	mi casa	7:00

Nombre: ______________________________ Fecha: ______________________________

ALGO MÁS: Some regular *-er* and *-ir* verbs

1-13 Las actividades de un estudiante. You will hear a student talk about himself and his activities. Listen carefully and put an **X** in the appropriate column to indicate if the following activities are mentioned or not.

	Sí	*No*
1. Toma notas en las clases.	_____	_____
2. Lee y estudia en su casa.	_____	_____
3. Come en la cafetería.	_____	_____
4. Saca buenas notas.	_____	_____
5. Escribe en la computadora.	_____	_____
6. Baila en una discoteca.	_____	_____
7. Aprende mucho en sus clases.	_____	_____

Mosaicos

1-14 La vida estudiantil. You will hear three brief selections followed by some related statements. Put an **X** in the appropriate column to indicate whether each of the statements is true or false. Don't worry if there are some words you don't understand.

		Sí	*No*
1.	a.	_____	_____
	b.	_____	_____
	c.	_____	_____

		Sí	*No*
2.	a.	_____	_____
	b.	_____	_____
	c.	_____	_____
	d.	_____	_____
	e.	_____	_____

		Sí	*No*
3.	a.	_____	_____
	b.	_____	_____
	c.	_____	_____
	d.	_____	_____
	e.	_____	_____
	f.	_____	_____

Pronunciación

Enlace *(Linking)*

Listen carefully to the explanation of Spanish linking. Repeat each of the phrases and sentences after the speaker when asked to do so. Make sure to avoid any pauses between words.

Spanish words are typically linked together in normal speech. If a Spanish word ends in a consonant and the next word begins with a vowel, the consonant forms a syllable with the following vowel.

Repeat the following sentences, avoiding any pauses between the words. **Repitan las siguientes oraciones.**

1. Nosotros hablamos español.
2. Practicamos en la clase.
3. Ellos estudian español.
4. Ellas enseñan a las ocho.

Nombre: ______________________________ Fecha: ______________________________

If a word ends in **a**, **e**, or **o** and the next word begins with one of these vowels, but not an identical one, the resulting combination is linked. Repeat the following sentences, avoiding any pauses between the words. **Repitan las siguientes oraciones.**

1. Ana es optimista.
2. Paco está en la clase.
3. No habla español.

If a word ends in a vowel and the next word begins with the same vowel sound, the two vowels are linked in careful speech. In rapid speech, the two vowels are pronounced as one. Now you will hear the words linked in careful speech. Repeat the phrases avoiding any pauses between the words. **Repitan las siguientes frases.**

una amiga americana   ocho horas   estudia alemán

Now you will hear the same words in rapid speech. Note that the two vowels are pronounced as one. **Escuchen.**

una amiga americana   ocho horas   estudia alemán

When two words are linked by any combination of **a**, **e**, or **o** with **i** or **u**, the vowels form a diphthong which is pronounced as one syllable.

Repeat the following words pronouncing the vowel combinations as one syllable. **Repitan las siguientes frases.**

mi amigo   la universidad   la historia   habla inglés

Lección 2

Los amigos hispanos

A PRIMERA VISTA

2-1 Cuatro personas. You will hear a number followed by the description of a person. Write the appropriate number in the space provided below each person's picture. Don't worry if there are some words you don't understand.

___

___

___

___

2-2 ¿Cómo son estas personas? You will hear descriptions of five persons. Write the appropriate number next to the name of each person.

	Persona	País	Descripción
_____	Felipe Barba	México	alto, simpático, tiene bigote
_____	Andrea Cano	Argentina	inteligente, activa, habladora
_____	Andrés Arias	Panamá	gordo, viejo, inteligente
_____	Elías Ponce	Colombia	moreno, trabajador, soltero
_____	Carmen Anaya	Puerto Rico	alta, tiene 20 años, agradable
_____	Irene Álvarez	Perú	joven, bonita, casada
_____	Catalina Rivera	Venezuela	rubia, alegre, tiene 22 años

2-3 Autodescripción. You will hear a young man and a young woman describe themselves. Fill in the chart as you hear the information.

	Nombre	Nacionalidad	Edad	Descripción	Lugar
Chico					
Chica					

2-4 ¿Sí o no? You will hear a conversation between friends. Listen carefully, then indicate whether the statements below are true or false by checking **sí** or **no.**

	Sí	*No*
1. La amiga de Rafael se llama Antonia.	_____	_____
2. Ella es de Guatemala.	_____	_____
3. Estudia en la universidad este semestre.	_____	_____
4. Tiene trece años.	_____	_____
5. Ella desea ser profesora de inglés.	_____	_____

Explicación y expansión

Adjectives

2-5 Una comedia. Listen to the description of a play and the people involved in it. Circle the form of the adjective corresponding to the description.

1. excelente / excelentes
2. simpático / simpática / simpáticos / simpáticas
3. bonito / bonita / bonitos / bonitas
4. joven / jóvenes
5. nervioso / nerviosa / nerviosos / nerviosas
6. contento / contenta / contentos / contentas

2-6 Descripciones. You will hear a description of six students. Fill in the chart below as you hear the information.

Nombres	Aspecto físico	Personalidad
Marcela		
Ernesto		
Amelia y Marta		
Arturo y José		

Nombre: ______________________ Fecha: ______________________

Present tense and some uses of the verb *ser*

2-7 Hora y lugar. What's going on in Puebla? Write down the time and place of each event.

MODELO: You see: la fiesta
You hear: La fiesta es a la una en el parque.
You write: *a la una en el parque*

	La hora	*El lugar*
1. el concierto	________	________
2. la conferencia *(lecture)*	________	________
3. el baile	________	________
4. el banquete	________	________
5. el concurso *(contest)*	________	________

Ser and *estar* with adjectives

2-8 Información. Listen as Professor López asks the class for information about some students. Then write the number of each question below the verb form you would use to answer it.

es	está	están	son

Question words

2-9 Entrevista. You are being interviewed by your school newspaper. Answer each question appropriately. If necessary, stop the tape after each question to give your response.

2-10 Datos sobre Carlos. Complete the chart below with questions and answers based on the description you hear. You may listen to the description as many times as you wish.

Preguntas	Respuestas
¿Cómo se llama el chico?	
	Es norteamericano.
¿Cómo es?	
	En un gimnasio.
¿A qué hora llega al trabajo?	

ALGO MÁS: Expressions with *gustar*

2-11 Las novelas. Listen to an interview concerning a writer's likes and dislikes. Indicate her preferences by putting an **X** in the appropriate columns in the tables below.

Actividades	Le gusta	No le gusta
leer		
escribir por las mañanas		
escuchar música clásica		

Novelas	Le gustan	No le gustan
históricas		
románticas		
de misterio		

Nombre: ______________________ Fecha: ______________________

MOSAICOS

2-12 Un estudiante de intercambio. You will hear two friends talking about Miguel Hernández Colón, an exchange student. As you listen, try to find out his nationality, age, and what kind of person he is. Then mark the correct answers.

1. Miguel es

a._____ panameño. b._____ colombiano. c._____ chileno.

2. Tiene

a._____ 18 años. b._____ 22 años. c._____ 25 años.

3. Es un chico

a._____ fuerte, pero perezoso. b._____ alegre y listo. c._____ callado y trabajador.

2-13 ¿Quién? ¿Qué? ¿Dónde? You will hear three short conversations. For each one write down the names of the persons, what they are doing or are going to do, and where they are. Play the tape again, if necessary, to check what you have written.

Personas	Actividad	Lugar
0. *Ángela, Ernesto*	*escuchar*	*laboratorio*
1.		
2.		
3.		

PRONUNCIACIÓN

b, v, and d

b and v

In Spanish, the letters **b** and **v** are pronounced the same. At the beginning of an utterance or after an **m** or **n**, the Spanish **b** and **v** are pronounced like the English *b*. **Repitan las siguientes palabras.**

bien buenos bonito enviar combate vaca

In all other positions the Spanish **b** and **v** are pronounced by allowing air to pass between the lips, which are almost closed. This sound does not exist in English. **Repitan las siguientes palabras.**

sabe Cuba cabeza uva pavo aviso

The following words contain both pronunciations of **b** and **v** within the same words. **Repitan las siguientes palabras.**

bebe bebida vive bobo barbero víbora

d

The Spanish **d** has two pronunciations, depending on its position in a word or sentence. At the beginning of a sentence or after **l** or **n**, the Spanish **d** is pronounced by placing the tip of the tongue against the back of the upper teeth. The air flow is interrupted until the tongue is retracted. **Repitan las siguientes palabras.**

don donde doña doctor día dinero

In all other positions, the **d** is similar to the pronunciation of the English *th* in the word *father*. **Repitan las siguientes palabras.**

adiós comida saludos usted médico lado verdad

Stress and the written accent

Word stress is meaningful in both English and Spanish. In both languages all words generally have one stressed syllable. In some instances, a change in stress signals a change in meaning. For example, the English words *permit* and *present* may be stressed on either syllable. When the first syllable is stressed, these words are nouns. When the second syllable is stressed, they are verbs.

Nombre: ______________________ Fecha: ______________________

Noun	*Verb*
permit	permit
present	present

Now listen to the following sentence that uses both pronunciations of the word *permit.*

Without a parking permit, the police will not permit you to park here.

The differences in meaning due to stress are more common in Spanish than in English. One effect is to change the tense of a verb. Sometimes stress is indicated with a written accent.

Present: **hablo** *Past:* **habló**

Now listen to the following sentence that uses both pronunciations.

Yo **hablo** hoy; él **habló** ayer. *I speak today; he spoke yesterday.*

If you know how to pronounce a word, you can determine if it needs a written accent by applying a few simple rules. Similarly, if you read a word and know these rules, the presence or absence of a written accent will tell you where to place the stress. Beginning with this lesson, you will learn the rules for accentuation.
Rule 1. Interrogative and exclamatory words have a written accent on the vowel of the stressed syllable. For example, in the interrogative word **cómo,** a written accent is needed over the stressed **o** of the first syllable.

Dictado. Listen and then write the interrogative and exclamatory words you hear.

1. _____ 2. _____ 3. _____ 4. _____ 5. _____ 6. _____

Lección 3
Las actividades y los planes

A PRIMERA VISTA

3-1 Diversiones. Listen to two young people describing their leisure activities. Then, indicate whether the following statements are true or false by marking **sí** or **no.**

Descripción 1	*Sí*	*No*
1. Roberto va mucho al cine.	_____	_____
2. Los amigos de Roberto escuchan música en casa.	_____	_____
3. Roberto conversa con sus compañeros de la universidad.	_____	_____

Descripción 2	*Sí*	*No*
4. Elena toca la guitarra.	_____	_____
5. Ella canta canciones norteamericanas.	_____	_____
6. Elena baila en la discoteca los lunes y los miércoles.	_____	_____

3-2 ¿Qué haces? A classmate you just met would like to know your preferences with regard to different activities. Answer his questions according to the model.

MODELO: You hear: ¿Tocas la guitarra?
You say: *Sí, toco la guitarra.* o *No, no toco la guitarra.*

3-3 En un restaurante. Listen to Marisa and Javier ordering dinner at a restaurant, and then to the statements about their conversation with the waitress. For all statements that are true, check **sí**; for all statements that are false, check **no**.

	Sí	*No*
1.	_____	_____
2.	_____	_____
3.	_____	_____
4.	_____	_____
5.	_____	_____
6.	_____	_____

3-4 La merienda. You are studying in Madrid and normally have a snack in the afternoon at your favorite café. Respond appropriately to the waiter.

3-5 En el supermercado. Listen for the items that different persons plan to buy in the supermarket and write them below.

MODELO: You hear: Olga necesita espaguetis y tomates.
You write: *espaguetis, tomates*

1. Marta: ______________________________
2. Roberto: ______________________________
3. Ana: ______________________________
4. Sra. Martínez: ______________________________
5. Sra. Hernández: ______________________________
6. Las chicas: ______________________________
7. Sr. Padilla: ______________________________
8. Sara: ______________________________

EXPLICACIÓN Y EXPANSIÓN

Present tense of regular *-er* and *-ir* verbs

3-6 La dieta de Olga. Olga is on a diet to lose weight. Say whether she should eat or drink each of the following items.

MODELO: *Olga no debe comer pizza.*

1. ... 2. ... 3. ... 4. ...

Nombre: ______________________ Fecha: ______________________

3-7 A comer y beber. You and your friends are at a restaurant. Say what you are having according to the pictures and the cues you hear.

MODELOS: 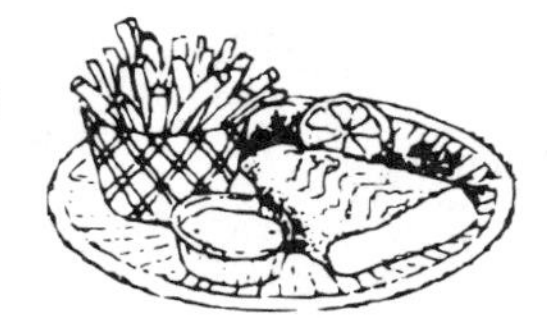

yo
Yo como pescado y papas fritas.

tú
Tú bebes café.

1. ...

2. ...

3. ...

4. ...

5. ...

3-8 ¿Dónde viven? Say where each person lives according to the cues you hear.

MODELO: Marina / México
Marina vive en México.

Present tense of *ir*

3-9 Los planes de Mónica. Listen to Mónica's plans for next week. Identify what she is going to do and when by writing the corresponding number under the correct day.

MODELO: 0. Mónica va a ir al cine el domingo.
(Mark "0" under Sunday the 17th.)

L	M	M	J	V	S	D
11	12	13	14	15	16	17

Ir + *a* + infinitive to express future action

3-10 Mis amigos y yo. Assuming that the pictures below show what you and your friends are going to do, tell what your plans are.

MODELO:  *Vamos a practicar en el gimnasio esta tarde.*

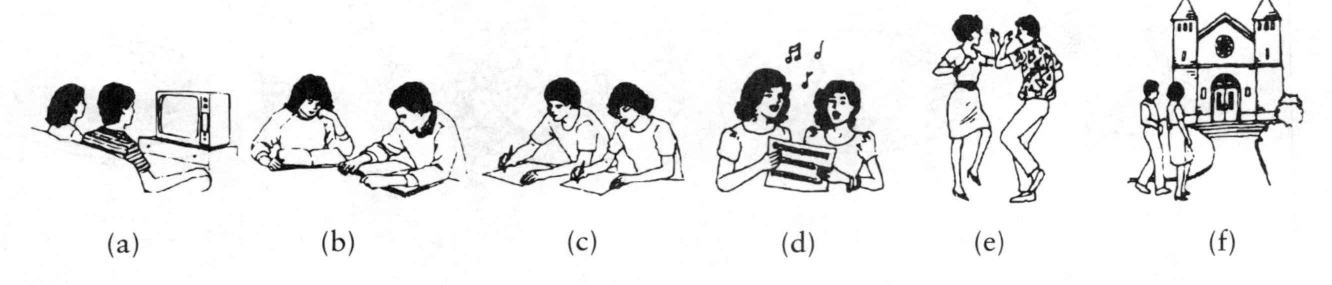

(a) (b) (c) (d) (e) (f)

Numbers 100 to 2,000,000

3-11 Identificación. You will hear only one number from each group below. Circle that number.

MODELO: You hear: ciento sesenta y tres
You see: 273 238 136 163
You write: (163)

1. 198 287 368 167
2. 104 205 405 504
3. 213 312 603 933
4. 416 624 704 914
5. 100 300 400 1.000

Nombre: ______________________________ Fecha: ______________________________

3-12 Los números. Listen to the numbers and repeat each one after the speaker. Then, write the number in Arabic numerals.

MODELO: You hear: trescientos treinta y seis
You write: *336*

1. _____ 5. _____ 8. _____

2. _____ 6. _____ 9. _____

3. _____ 7. _____ 10. _____

4. _____

ALGO MÁS: Some uses of *por* and *para*

3-13 ¿Por o para? You will hear various questions regarding a trip. Answer them by completing the following sentences with **por** or **para.**

1. Vamos _______________ Cartagena.
2. _______________ supuesto.
3. Vamos a nadar y a caminar _______________ la playa.
4. Vamos a estar _______________ cinco días

MOSAICOS

3-14 Las vacaciones de Lola y Paco. Lola and Paco are discussing a travel package to Mexico City. Listen to their conversation and complete the chart with questions and answers based on the information you hear.

Preguntas	Respuestas
¿Dónde está el hotel?	
	Siete días.
¿Cuánto cuesta el viaje?	
	Van a bailar y a escuchar música típica.
¿Qué va a hacer Lola?	
	Van a comer pescado fresco.
¿Qué van a beber Paco y Lola?	

PRONUNCIACIÓN

Las consonantes g, j, r, and rr

Listen carefully to the explanation of how these Spanish consonants are pronounced. Repeat each word after the speaker when asked to do so.

g and j

At the beginning of an utterance or after **n**, the Spanish **g** when followed by **l, r, a, o,** or **u** is pronounced like the English *g* in *garden.* **Repitan las siguientes palabras.**

gata gusto goma gracias globo domingo

In all other positions, the Spanish **g** when followed by **l, r, a, o,** or **u** is pronounced with no interruption to the air flow, similar to the rapid and relaxed pronunciation of English *g* in *sugar.* **Repitan las siguientes palabras.**

amigo lugar regular lechuga agrupar la gata

In the syllables **gue** and **gui,** the letter **g** is pronounced as above, but the **u** is not pronounced. **Repitan las siguientes palabras.**

guerra guitarra guía Miguel seguir llegue

Nombre: ________________________ Fecha: ________________________

In Spanish, the pronunciation of the letter **g** in the syllables **ge** and **gi** and the letter **j** is very similar to the pronunciation of English *h* in the word *heel.* **Repitan las siguientes palabras.**

general ligero gigante viaje joya jueves

r and rr

In Spanish, whenever the letter **r** occurs between vowels or after a consonant, its pronunciation is similar to the English *d, dd, t,* or *tt* in words such as *matter, water*, or *ladder* when pronounced rapidly by an American. **Repitan las siguientes palabras.**

pero señora dinero pared tres otro

The Spanish **r** at the beginning of a word, after **n** or **l,** and **rr** are pronounced by placing the tip of the tongue on the upper ridge of the gum and tapping it several times. This sound does not exist in English. **Repitan las siguientes palabras.**

perro carro rico Roberto Enrique regalo

Stress and the written accent

Rule 2. All words that are stressed on the third syllable from the end of the word must have a written accent. **Repitan las siguientes palabras.**

física sábado simpático gramática matemáticas

Say each of the following words aloud, stressing the third-from-the-last syllable. Note that each word has a written accent. You will hear a confirmation after you say each word.

1. artículo
2. bolígrafo
3. número
4. informática
5. párrafo
6. antipático
7. cómodo
8. película
9. teléfono
10. cronómetro

Lección 4
La familia

A PRIMERA VISTA

4-1 La familia de Paloma. Look at Paloma's family tree. You will hear a number followed by a word identifying the relationship of a person in the family tree to Paloma. Write the number next to that person's name.

MODELO: You hear: 0. abuelo
You write: *0 next to the name don Felipe.*

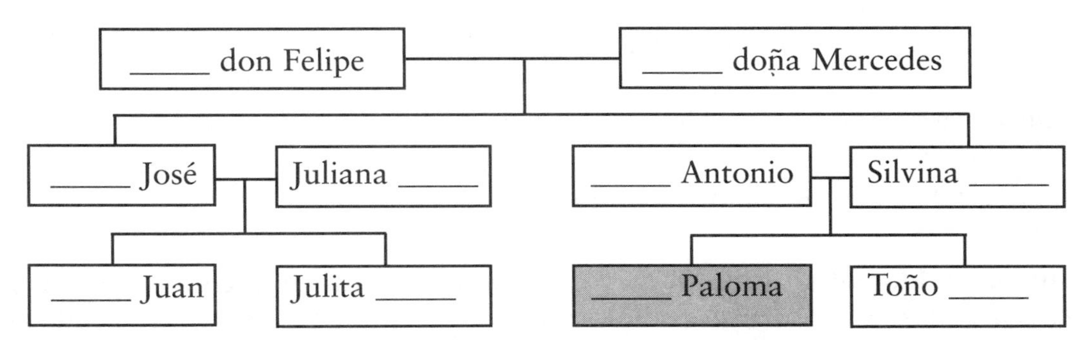

4-2 Familiares de mis compañeros. Repeat each statement after the speaker. Then write the number of relatives mentioned and their relationship to the person named.

MODELO: You hear: Rafael tiene dos hermanos.
You write: *dos hermanos*

1. Rosa ____________
2. Elena ____________
3. Rosendo ____________
4. Clarita ____________
5. Carlos ____________
6. Pepe ____________
7. Marina ____________
8. Juan ____________

4-3 La familia de Alicia. You will hear Alicia Ramos Jaramillo describing her family. Identify each family relationship to Alicia by writing it next to the appropriate name.

1. Carlos Ramos Mendoza ____________
2. Arturo ____________
3. Pedrito ____________
4. Juan Carlos ____________
5. Mónica Jaramillo ____________
6. Alicia Jaramillo de Ramos ____________

4-4 El bautizo. Baptism is a very important celebration in most Spanish and Latin American homes. Listen to the description of the baptism (**el bautizo**) of a new member of the Romero family. Then, indicate whether each statement is true or false by marking the appropriate response. Don't worry if you don't understand every word.

	Sí	*No*
1. Los Romero van a celebrar el bautizo de su primer hijo.	_____	_____
2. El niño se llama Fernando José por su padrino.	_____	_____
3. Los abuelos van a ser los padrinos.	_____	_____
4. El bautizo va a ser en la casa de los Romero.	_____	_____
5. La familia y los amigos van a ir al bautizo.	_____	_____

4-5 La familia de Florentino Rodríguez. An exchange student from Uruguay is talking to a group of friends about his family. Complete the chart with the information you hear. (You won't be able to fill in every block.) You may listen to the tape as many times as necessary.

Nombre(s)	Parentesco	Edad	Trabajo	¿Cómo es (son)?
	padre			
			en un banco	
Pedro				
				muy lista
		28 años		
			estudiantes	
Juan Díaz				
				tranquila
León				

Nombre: ______________________________ Fecha: ______________________________

EXPLICACIÓN Y EXPANSIÓN

Present tense of stem-changing verbs *(e>ie, o>ue, e>i)*

4-6 La hora de empezar. You are in charge of a school radio program. Use the cues to answer your classmate's questions about when the people participating in the program are scheduled to begin.

MODELO: You hear: ¿A qué hora empieza Pepito?
You see: 10:00
You say: *Empieza a las diez.*

1. 11:00 2. 10:30 3. 12:00 4. 1:00 5. 9:00

4-7 Preferimos Cancún. A group of friends who will spend their vacation in Guadalajara all prefer to go to Cancún. Express that preference by completing each of the speaker's statements.

MODELO: El señor Gómez va a ir a Guadalajara.
Pero él prefiere ir a Cancún.

4-8 ¿Cuántas horas duermen? According to the times given, say how many hours you and your friends sleep.

MODELO: You see: Mirta / 8
You say: *Mirta duerme ocho horas.*

1. Juan y Miguel / 6
2. La señora Sánchez / 7
3. nosotros / 9
4. tú / 10
5. yo / 8

4-9 Sirven fajitas. Listen to this conversation and to the questions that follow. Circle the best answer based on what you hear.

1. a) en la cocina b) en un restaurante c) en una escuela
2. a) su hermano b) su padre c) un amigo
3. a) arroz con pollo b) tacos c) fajitas
4. a) fajitas b) enchiladas c) tacos
5. a) vino blanco b) cerveza c) agua

4-10 La fiesta del Club de Español. You are organizing a party for the Spanish Club. Using the cues you hear, tell what each of these people is getting for the party.

MODELO: María / el estéreo
María consigue el estéreo.

Expressions with *tener*

4-11 Situaciones. Listen to these descriptions of people in various situations. Give the expression with **tener** that best completes each description.

1. Tiene calor.	Tiene sueño.
2. Tiene hambre.	Tiene cuidado.
3. Tienen dos años.	Tienen miedo.
4. Tiene sed.	Tiene prisa.
5. Tiene suerte.	Tiene frío.

4-12 Para el examen de mañana. Tell what these people must do before tomorrow's Spanish test.

MODELO: You see: María Antonieta / escuchar los casetes
You say: *María Antonieta tiene que escuchar los casetes.*

1. Jorge / ir al laboratorio
2. nosotros / leer las lecciones
3. los estudiantes / practicar los diálogos
4. tú / estudiar el vocabulario
5. yo / escribir los números

4-13 Preguntas personales. Answer the five questions you will hear appropriately.

Possessive adjectives

4-14 ¿Cuál es el adjetivo? Listen to the speaker's statements about his family and then write the possessive adjective you hear.

MODELO: You hear: Mis padres son de Colombia.
You write: *mis*

1. ______________
2. ______________
3. ______________
4. ______________
5. ______________
6. ______________

4-15 ¿De quién es? Answer a friend's questions about people's possessions negatively, using possessive adjectives.

MODELO: You hear: ¿Es el auto de Ángel?
You say: *No, no es su auto.*

Present tense of *hacer, poner, salir, traer,* and *oír*

4-16 Un día difícil. Pancho is trying to get ready for school but his mother needs his help. Listen to their conversation and then read the statements below. If the statement is true, check **sí**. If the statement is false, check **no**.

	Sí	*No*
1. Pancho está en casa.	_____	_____
2. Pancho hace la cama.	_____	_____
3. La madre prepara el desayuno.	_____	_____
4. Pancho pone la mesa.	_____	_____
5. La madre sale a las ocho.	_____	_____

4-17 Yo también. Your mother wants you to help out more at home and is pointing out the chores that your brothers and sisters do. Tell her that you also do these chores.

MODELO: You hear: Ellos ponen la mesa.
You say: *Yo pongo la mesa también.*

ALGO MÁS: Hace with expressions of time

4-18 ¿Cuánto tiempo hace? You will hear a brief description of a boy and his activities. Before listening to the description, look at the chart below. Then, as you listen to the description, put an **X** in the appropriate column.

	2 meses	**6 meses**	**3 años**	**5 años**	**8 años**
1. Agustín vive en la misma casa hace					
2. Estudia en la Escuela Moderna hace					
3. Tiene un perro hace					
4. Tiene una bicicleta hace					

Nombre: ______________________________ Fecha: ______________________________

Mosaicos

4-19 Planes para Francisco. Listen to Francisco's and his uncle's plans, and to the statements that follow. Indicate whether each statement is true or false by checking the appropriate response. Don't worry if you don't understand every word.

	Sí	*No*
1.	_____	_____
2.	_____	_____
3.	_____	_____
4.	_____	_____
5.	_____	_____

4-20 ¿Qué quieren? Pedrito and his sister Elena are discussing their family's plans for the weekend. Complete the chart with the information you hear about each family member's preferences.

¿Quién?	¿Qué quiere?
	Él quiere ir a la playa.
Pedrito	
Elenita	
	Quiere tomar el sol y leer un libro.
los abuelos	

Pronunciación

l, m, n, and ñ

l

At the beginning of a syllable, the pronunciation of the Spanish and English **l** is very similar. At the end of a syllable, the Spanish **l** has the same pronunciation, while English *l* is quite different. Compare the pronunciation of the following words: **Lucas**, *Lucas*; **hotel**, *hotel*. **Repitan las siguientes palabras.**

lápiz   libro   mal   papel   el   español   alto

m and n

The Spanish and English **m** are pronounced the same. **Repitan las siguientes palabras.**

mamá malo amable moreno mesa mexicano

At the beginning of a syllable, Spanish and English **n** are pronounced the same. At the end of a syllable, however, the Spanish **n** may vary according to consonant that follows it. Before **p, b,** and **v,** the Spanish **n** is pronounced like an **m;** before **g , k , j, q, ca, co,** and **cu,** the Spanish **n** is pronounced like **ng. Repitán las siguientes palabras.**

noche un bolígrafo un viejo un periódico un japonés inglés
un casete un cohete encuesta

ñ

The Spanish **ñ** is similar to the pronunciation of *ni* in the English word *onion* or *ny* in *canyon*. Listen and repeat the following words.

español señora mañana pequeño tamaño

Stress and the written accent

Rule 3. Words that are stressed on the next-to-last syllable do not have a written accent if they end in **n, s,** or a vowel. They do have a written accent if they end in any other letter. **Repitan las siguientes palabras.**

e**xa**men **ca**sas **pa**dre her**ma**na so**bri**no co**ci**no

Read the following words that stress the next-to-last syllable. Note that they do not have a written accent because they end in **n, s,** or a vowel. You will hear a confirmation after you have read each word.

1. butaca
2. lavabo
3. garaje
4. batidora
5. lejos
6. tareas
7. espejos
8. dientes
9. alquilan
10. hacen

Remember that words that are stressed on the next-to-last syllable have an accent mark if they do not end in **n**, **s**, or a vowel. **Repitan las siguientes palabras.**

lápiz útil débil mártir Félix carácter

Read the following words stressing the next-to-last syllable. Note that all these words have a written accent because they do not end in **n**, **s**, or a vowel. You will hear a confirmation after you have read each word.

1. fácil
2. suéter
3. álbum
4. Bolívar
5. sándwich
6. portátil
7. Velázquez
8. difícil

Lección 5
La casa y los muebles

A PRIMERA VISTA

5-1 La casa de la familia Hurtado. Listen to the description of the Hurtado family's house. Then, indicate whether each statement below is true or false by marking the appropriate response. Don't worry if you don't understand every word.

	Sí	*No*
1. La casa de la familia Hurtado es pequeña.	_____	_____
2. La casa tiene dos pisos.	_____	_____
3. El dormitorio de los padres está en el primer piso.	_____	_____
4. Los Hurtado tienen solo un hijo.	_____	_____
5. La abuelita vive con su familia.	_____	_____
6. La casa de los Hurtado tiene dos dormitorios.	_____	_____

5-2 ¿En qué parte de la casa están? Listen as the speaker names various pieces of furniture and appliances. Say in what room of the house each is normally found.

MODELO: You hear: el horno
You say: *El horno está en la cocina.*

5-3 El apartamento de Ana María. Ana María Salazar is moving into the apartment shown below. Look at the layout and write the name of each piece of furniture or appliance mentioned in the space provided next to the appropriate room. You may listen to the tape more than once.

dormitorio

____

____

____

____

____

____

closet

____

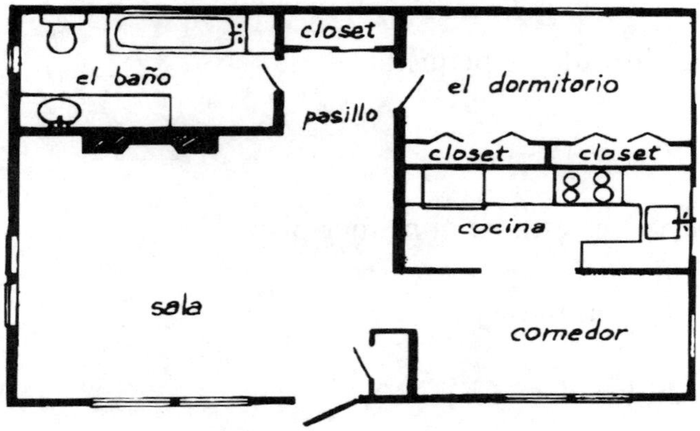

____

cocina

____

____

sala

____

____

____

comedor

____

____

5-4 Un matrimonio moderno. Listen as Amanda and Tomás discuss their chores while preparing dinner. Then listen to the statements that follow and indicate in the chart who is doing each chore mentioned.

	1	2	3	4	5	6
Amanda						
Tomás						

Nombre: ______________________________ Fecha: ______________________________

5-5 ¿Qué hacen Sandra y Felipe el sábado? Sandra lives in an apartment, and Felipe lives in a dorm. Listen as a friend describes what they do on Saturday. Complete the chart with the information you hear.

Actividades		
Hora	**Sandra**	**Felipe**
8:00 a.m.		
9:30 a.m.		
10:30 a.m.		
3:00 p.m.		
5:30 p.m.		
por la noche		

5-6 Preguntas personales. Answer your sociology instructor's questions about which members of your family do these chores in your home.

MODELO: You hear: ¿Quién barre la casa?
You say: *Mi hermano barre la casa.*

EXPLICACIÓN Y EXPANSIÓN

Present progressive

5-7 Ana está hablando con su tía. While Ernesto is at his friend Ana's home, her aunt calls. Listen to Ana's side of the conversation and indicate what each person mentioned is doing by matching each numbered item in the left-hand column with the appropriate activity on the right.

Persona	*Actividad*
1. La madre _____	a. Está conversando con un amigo.
2. El abuelo _____	b. Está lavando los platos.
3. Ana _____	c. Está estudiando para un examen.
4. La abuela _____	d. Está durmiendo en su cuarto.
5. El padre _____	e. Está sacando la basura.

5-8 Pero hoy no. . . People tend to be creatures of habit who do the same things at the same time. But today is different. Explain in Spanish that today these people aren't doing what they normally do.

MODELO: Ana María simpre camina por la mañana.
Pero hoy no está caminando.

Direct object nouns and pronouns

5-9 Sí, mamá. . . Answer your mother's questions about who does various chores, using direct object pronouns.

MODELO: ¿José lava el auto?
Sí, mamá, José lo lava.

5-10 Los problemas de Carlos. Carlos received low grades this semester. Answer his father's questions in the negative using direct object pronouns.

MODELO: ¿Estudia Carlos las lecciones?
No, no las estudia.

Nombre: ______________________ Fecha: ______________________

5-11 Preguntas personales. A new friend is inquiring about your activities. Answer using direct object pronouns.

MODELO: ¿Limpias tu cuarto?
Sí, lo limpio (o *No, no lo limpio*).

5-12 ¿Qué van a hacer? Answer the following questions about your activities with your friends using direct object pronouns.

MODELO: ¿Van a escribir la lección?
Sí, vamos a escribirla (o *No, no vamos a escribirla*).

Demonstrative adjectives

5-13 ¿Cerca o lejos? You hear the following comments at a furniture store. Indicate with an **X** in the appropriate row of the chart whether the objects and persons mentioned are next to the speaker (**al lado**), a short distance from the speaker (**cerca**), or relatively far from the speaker (**lejos**).

MODELO: You hear: Ese espejo es muy pequeño para el baño.
*(You would put an **X** in the row labeled **cerca**.)*

	1	2	3	4	5	6
al lado						
cerca						
lejos						

5-14 Un amigo me pregunta. Answer a friend's questions using the cues below and the appropriate form of **este,** according to the model.

MODELO: You hear: ¿Qué prefieres?
You see: libro
You say: *Prefiero este libro.*

1. revista
2. electrodomésticos
3. sábanas
4. jabón
5. toallas

5-15 ¿En qué lugar? You are helping out a friend who is new to the area. Answer his questions using the correct form of **ese** and the cues provided.

MODELO: You hear: ¿Dónde vive Alfredo?
You see: casa
You say: *En esa casa.*

1. oficina
2. café
3. librería
4. parque
5. edificios

Demonstrative pronouns

5-16 Quiero aquélla. Answer a friend's questions about your preferences using the correct form of **aquél.**

MODELO: ¿Quieres esta computadora o ésa?
Quiero aquélla.

Saber and *conocer (to know)*

5-17 Buscando trabajo. Your friend Ernesto is applying for a summer job. Listen to his conversation with a prospective employer, and mark the verb that best completes each statement in the chart based on what you hear.

Conoce	Sabe	
_____	_____	a varios estudiantes
_____	_____	usar computadoras
_____	_____	que tiene que trabajar 30 horas a la semana
_____	_____	español, inglés y francés
_____	_____	al profesor González

Nombre: ______________________ Fecha: ______________________

5-18 Conozco a Miguel Zorrilla. Use **saber** or **conocer** and the cues to tell what you know about a new Chilean student.

MODELOS: Miguel Zorrilla
Conozco a Miguel Zorrilla.
dónde vive
Sé dónde vive.

ALGO MÁS: More on adjectives

5-19 ¿En qué piso? Listen to the following inquiries at the information center of an important department store. Put an **X** in the appropriate column according to the answers given. Don't worry if there are some words you don't understand.

Conversación	piso 1	piso 2	piso 3	piso 4	piso 5	piso 6
1						
2						
3						

MOSAICOS

5-20 Una reunión familiar. Your neighbors, the Arizas, are busy getting ready for a family reunion. Listen to what they are doing and the statements that follow. Then indicate whether each statement is true or false by putting an **X** in the appropriate column.

	Sí	*No*
1.	_____	_____
2.	_____	_____
3.	_____	_____
4.	_____	_____
5.	_____	_____

PRONUNCIACIÓN

Ll, y, and x

ll and y

In most parts of the Spanish-speaking world, **y** and **ll** are pronounced like the English *y* in the word *yoke*, but with more friction. At the end of a word, **y** sounds very similar to the Spanish **i**, but if the next word begins with a vowel, **y** is pronounced like English *y* in *yoke*. **Repitan las siguientes palabras.**

yo   llamo   ella   calle   estoy   muy bien   muy alto

x

Before a consonant, the Spanish **x** is pronounced like the English *ks* or *s*. **Repitan las siguientes palabras.**

experiencia   explicación   experimento   texto   extensión

Between vowels, **x** is pronounced like **ks**. It is never pronounced like the English *x*.

examen   sexo   existir   exacto   éxito

Nombre: ______________________ Fecha: ______________________

Stress and the written accent

Rule 4. Words that are stressed on the last syllable have an accent mark if they end in **n, s,** or a vowel. They do not have an accent mark if they end in any other letter. **Repitan las siguientes palabras.**

est**án** est**ás** est**á** ingl**és** alem**án** auto**bús**

Read the following words. Note that these words do have a written accent because they end in **n, s,** or a vowel and are stressed on the last syllable. You will hear a confirmation after you have read each word. **¿Listos? Empecemos.**

1. francés 2. portugués 3. café 4. jabón 5. bebé 6. esquí
7. atún 8. perdón

Remember that these words do not have a written accent in the plural form because the stress falls on the next-to-last syllable. **Repitan las siguientes palabras.**

japonés japoneses alemán alemanes autobús autobuses
jabón jabones

Remember that words that are stressed on the last syllable do not have a written accent if they end in any letter except **n, s,** or a vowel. **Repitan las siguientes palabras.**

hablar verdad español feliz borrador

Read the following words that are stressed on the last syllable. Note that they do not have a written accent. You will hear a confirmation after you have read each word.

1. vegetal 2. pared 3. alquilar 4. azul 5. borrador
6. terminar 7. papel 8. universidad

Lección 6

El tiempo y los deportes

A PRIMERA VISTA

6-1 ¿Qué deporte practican? You will hear three brief conversations about sports. After each conversation, put an **X** in the column corresponding to the appropriate sport. Don't worry if there are words you don't understand.

Conversación	béisbol	ciclismo	esquí	fútbol	golf	tenis
1						
2						
3						

6-2 El tiempo. Listen to these two descriptions of college students' vacation plans. Then, indicate whether the statements below are true or false by marking the appropriate responses. Don't worry if you don't understand every word.

Descripción 1	*Sí*	*No*
1. Jorge piensa jugar al fútbol con sus amigos.	_____	_____
2. Según la televisión, va a hacer buen tiempo este fin de semana.	_____	_____
3. Patricio y Jorge van a salir el jueves por la mañana.	_____	_____
4. Piensan volver el domingo después de las siete.	_____	_____

Descripción 2	*Sí*	*No*
1. Victoria quiere ir a la playa.	_____	_____
2. Es verano y hace mucho calor.	_____	_____
3. Ella llama a su mamá.	_____	_____
4. Victoria va a salir con Ana María esta tarde.	_____	_____

6-3 Pronóstico del tiempo. On a shortwave radio, you hear the following weather forecasts from different parts of the world. Indicate in the chart which sport or sports people could play in each place according to the weather report for their area.

Deportes	1	2	3	4	5	6
béisbol						
ciclismo						
esquí						
basquetbol						
fútbol						
voleibol						

EXPLICACIÓN Y EXPANSIÓN

Preterit tense of regular verbs

6-4 Vacaciones en la playa. A friend is telling you about a decision her relatives made while on vacation in South America. Listen to the story and then indicate whether each statement is true or false by marking **sí** or **no** below.

	Sí	*No*
1. Los tíos pasaron las vacaciones en Uruguay.	_____	_____
2. Ellos asistieron a varios partidos de béisbol en Montevideo.	_____	_____
3. La tía Gloria nadó mucho en la playa.	_____	_____
4. Ellos compraron una casa muy grande en la playa.	_____	_____
5. La casa tiene cuatro dormitorios y una terraza.	_____	_____
6. Piensan alquilar el apartamento algunos meses del año.	_____	_____

Nombre: ______________________________ Fecha: ______________________________

6-5 Ayer. . . You will hear statements about what various people are going to do. Contradict each statement, explaining that they did the activities yesterday.

MODELO: Manola y Asunción van a comprar un refrigerador hoy.
No, compraron un refrigerador ayer.

6-6 El detective. You are a detective who must watch a suspect and report his whereabouts. Looking at the list below, tell what the suspect did yesterday morning and early in the afternoon.

MODELO: hablar por teléfono a las siete
Habló por teléfono a las siete.

1. desayunar a las ocho
2. salir de su casa después
3. visitar a su hija a las diez
4. jugar con su nieto
5. almorzar con su hija
6. volver a su casa a las dos

Preterit of *ir* and *ser*

6-7 El abuelo. Your grandfather is reminiscing about a trip he made to Cuba as a young man. Complete the following paragraph with the missing words according to what you hear.

El abuelo visitó Cuba en el año ______________. Él ______________ a La Habana, la capital de Cuba, para pasar unas ______________ con la familia de un ______________. En la ciudad, el abuelo ______________ muchos lugares históricos. Él y su amigo ______________ a una fiesta en un club y después ______________ a ver el Malecón, una avenida muy bonita que está frente al mar. El abuelo piensa que ese viaje ______________ extraordinario.

6-8 ¿Adónde fueron? You have a dinner party at your home. A friend arrives early and finds that you are the only one at home. Tell your friend where your family members went according to the cues.

MODELO: madre / comprar una lechuga
Mi madre fue a comprar una lechuga.

Reflexive verbs and pronouns

6-9 Por la mañana. Looking at the times given, tell when each person gets up.

MODELO: Juan // 7:00
Juan se levanta a las siete.

1. Alicia / 7:30
2. Juan y Pedro / 8:00
3. yo / 9:00
4. mi padre / 6:00
5. nosotros / 9:00

6-10 Mi hermano y yo. A friend is telling you what he does at a summer resort. Tell your friend that you and your family do the same things.

MODELO: Yo me levanto a las siete.
Nosotros también nos levantamos a las siete.

6-11 Preguntas personales. Answer the questions on the tape about what you did this morning. Use complete sentences.

Adverbs

6-12 Pablito conversa con su tío. Listen to this conversation between Pablito and his uncle. Then choose the best answer for the following statements according to the information in the conversation.

1. a) diariamente b) dos veces a la semana c) muy poco
2. a) tranquilamente b) rápidamente c) lentamente
3. a) una hora b) dos horas c) cuarenta minutos
4. a) ganar el campeonato b) buscar más jugadores c) terminar en tercer lugar

6-13 Un accidente de tráfico. You will hear some sentences describing a traffic accident. Each sentence will be followed by a cue. Incorporate the cue into the sentence using the ending **-mente.**

MODELO: Los pasajeros esperaron. . .(paciente)
Los pasajeros esperaron pacientemente.

Preterit of *-er* and *-ir* verbs whose stem ends in a vowel and of stem-changing *-ir* verbs

6-14 El examen de español. Use the cues to tell what the students in Spanish 100 did yesterday to prepare for today's test.

MODELO: pedir unos casetes
Pidieron unos casetes.

6-15 Pero hoy no. Use the cues to explain that the people named did something different today from what they normally do.

MODELO: Pedro siempre pide pollo frito. / espagueti
Pero hoy pidió espagueti.

ALGO MÁS: Hace meaning *ago*

6-16 En Bariloche. While visiting Bariloche, you decide to go on a boat ride in the Nahuel Huapi lake. Assuming that it is now ten in the morning, as you hear the names of your fellow passengers, look at the time each person arrived at the dock and say how long ago they arrived.

MODELO: You see: Juan / 9:40
You say: *Juan llegó hace veinte minutos.*

1. Elvira / 9:50
2. Agustín y Carmen / 9:58
3. Ignacio / 9:55
4. Los Rivas / 9:45
5. Manuel / 9:35

MOSAICOS

6-17 El día del viaje. Isabel and Fernando are leaving to spend two weeks in Panamá. Listen to their conversation and to the statements that follow. Indicate whether each statement is true or false by marking the appropriate response. Don't worry if you don't understand every word.

	Sí	*No*
1.	_____	_____
2.	_____	_____
3.	_____	_____
4.	_____	_____
5.	_____	_____
6.	_____	_____
7.	_____	_____

6-18 El partido de fútbol. Your friends Jorge and Adolfo are excited about going to an important soccer game. Listen to the story and complete the paragraph based on what you hear.

Esta tarde hace _______________ y Jorge _______________ ir al partido de fútbol, pero no _______________ dinero para comprar la entrada. Él _______________ verlo en la televisión. Un amigo de Jorge lo llama desde el _______________ porque _______________ entradas para el partido y quiere invitarlo. Jorge está muy contento y _______________ rápidamente para _______________ temprano al partido.

PRONUNCIACIÓN

Stress and the written accent

Rule 5. A written accent is also placed on one-syllable words to distinguish them from words with the same spelling but different meanings. For example, the word **el** meaning *the* has no written accent, but the word **él** meaning *he* does.

el	*the*	**él**	*he*
si	*if*	**sí**	*yes*
te	*(to) you*	**té**	*tea*
tu	*your*	**tú**	*you*

Dictado. Listen to the following sentences. Fill in the blanks with the correct words.

1. __________ trabajas con __________ padre.
2. Creo que __________ tiene __________ libro.
3. ¿Cómo __________ llamas?
4. __________ siempre tomas __________.
5. __________, yo vivo en esa calle.
6. __________ tienes dinero, podemos ir al cine.

Lección 7
La ropa y las tiendas

A PRIMERA VISTA

7-1 ¿Qué ropa compran? Listen to four descriptions of people buying clothes in a department store and circle the letters corresponding to the articles of clothing each person bought.

7-2 ¿Qué ropa llevan? As you listen to these descriptions of three people, check off the items each person is wearing.

1. Roberto	_____ suéter	_____ camisa	_____ traje de baño
	_____ traje	_____ abrigo	_____ zapatos negros
	_____ impermeable	_____ corbata de rayas	_____ calcetines
2. Sandra	_____ blusa	_____ camisa	_____ camiseta
	_____ traje	_____ falda	_____ traje de baño
	_____ sombrero	_____ sandalias	_____ zapatos tenis
3. Susana	_____ falda	_____ vestido	_____ camiseta
	_____ blusa	_____ chaqueta	_____ abrigo
	_____ sombrero	_____ medias	_____ zapatos

7-3 Ropa para las vacaciones. The speaker is helping you decide what to buy for a vacation in the mountains. Answer her questions according to each picture and the cue.

MODELO: ¿Qué necesitas por si hace frío?
Necesito un suéter.

Nombre: ______________________________ Fecha: ______________________________

7-4 Una conversación por teléfono. Listen to this conversation and then indicate whether the statements below are true or false by checking **sí** or **no.**

	Sí	*No*
1. Paula llama a Josefina para salir.	_____	_____
2. Paula quiere ir al cine esta tarde.	_____	_____
3. Hay unas rebajas muy buenas en un centro comercial.	_____	_____
4. Josefina quiere comprarle un regalo a una amiga.	_____	_____
5. Paula y Josefina van a ir de compras.	_____	_____

EXPLICACIÓN Y EXPANSIÓN

Indirect object nouns and pronouns

7-5 Los regalos de Navidad. Ernesto is going to buy Christmas gifts for his brothers and some of his friends. Complete the chart with the information you hear.

Persona	Regalo	Lugar donde compra
		una librería
	las entradas	
Ester		
		una tienda

7-6 Las preguntas de mi amigo. Your friend doubts that you would do certain things. Answer his questions in the affirmative using indirect object pronouns.

MODELO: ¿Escribir una carta? ¿Al presidente?
Sí, le escribo una carta al presidente.

7-7 ¿A quién le va a comprar un regalo? Your friend Marta is going to buy clothes for her friends and family. Using the cues you hear, say what she is going to buy for each person.

MODELO: José y Pepe / una camisa
Marta les va a comprar una camisa a José y Pepe.

The verb *dar*

7-8 Accesorios. Using the cues provided, answer a friend's questions about what you are giving to different people.

MODELO: ¿Qué le das a tu abuelo? / guantes
Le doy unos guantes.

Gustar and similar verbs

7-9 En una tienda. Listen to this conversation in a department store and to the five statements that follow it. Indicate whether each statement is true or false by checking **sí** or **no,** respectively.

	Sí	*No*
1.	_____	_____
2.	_____	_____
3.	_____	_____
4.	_____	_____
5.	_____	_____

7-10 ¿Qué le gusta? Find out whether the person you have just met at a party likes or dislikes the following things.

MODELO: la música moderna
¿Te gusta la música moderna?

7-11 A Arturo le encantan los deportes. Tell a new acquaintance how much your friend Arturo loves all kinds of sports and games. Listen to the model sentence and to how it changes. Then repeat the first sentence and change it as necessary according to the cues.

MODELO: A Arturo le encanta esquiar.
los partidos de fútbol
A Arturo le encantan los partidos de fútbol.

Pronouns after prepositions

7-12 ¿Quién va con quién? Patricia is on the phone with her friend Irma making plans for a high school reunion. Listen to Patricia's side of the conversation and fill out the chart indicating with whom the following people are going.

	Irma	*Patricia*
1. Gregorio	_____	_____
2. los Gómez	_____	_____
3. la profesora Buendía	_____	_____
4. Amanda	_____	_____
5. Ana	_____	_____
6. Carlos	_____	_____

Some irregular preterits

7-13 Dos amigas hablan de Pepe. Listen to the conversation between two friends, Josefa and Elena, in the cafeteria. Then choose the best completion to the statements that follow, according to what you hear.

1. Pepe está en. . .
   a) el estadio. b) el hospital. c) una fiesta.
2. Josefa piensa. . ..
   a) visitar a Pepe. b) ir a un partido de fútbol. c) ir de compras.
3. Josefa conoció a María Paz en. . .
   a) el hospital. b) la oficina. c) la facultad de Medicina.
4. María Paz es. . .
   a) la novia de Pepe. b) la médica de Pepe. c) una profesora de la universidad.
5. Josefa invita a Elena a ir. . .
   a) a la facultad. b) al hospital. c) al estadio.

7-14 El Sr. Pérez habla con una colega. Listen to this conversation between Mr. Pérez and a business partner. Then circle the best answer to each question you hear.

1. a) En la universidad b) En una oficina
   c) En la clase

2. a) Tuvo que llamar a los estudiantes. b) Tuvo que dirigir una discusión.
   c) Tuvo que ir al banco.

3. a) Enseñar b) Estudiar
   c) Discutir con el Sr. Pérez

4. a) La economía del Japón b) Problemas económicos norteamericanos
   c) El comercio con México

7-15 El trabajo de Isabel. You will hear Isabel Gómez describing her day at work and statements that follow. Indicate whether each statement is true or false by marking the appropriate response

	Sí	*No*
1. Isabel Gómez Verdeja trabaja en una cafetería.	_____	_____
2. Isabel hizo muchas cosas ayer.	_____	_____
3. Su primera clienta almorzó a las dos de la tarde.	_____	_____
4. Isabel tuvo que traducir en su trabajo ayer.	_____	_____
5. Los clientes sudamericanos gastaron mucho dinero ayer.	_____	_____
6. Isabel cocinó cuando llegó a su casa.	_____	_____

7-16 En casa. Your mother is upset because everything is out of place. Answer her questions following the model and using the cues below.

MODELO: ¿Dónde puso tu padre la billetera?
la mesa de noche
La puso en la mesa de noche.

1. la sala 2. el escritorio 3. el comedor 4. el garaje 5. su cuarto

Nombre: ______________________ Fecha: ______________________

7-17 Preguntas personales. You will hear four questions about your last vacation. Answer the questions by telling either what you actually did or what you would have done during your ideal vacation.

ALGO MÁS: Some uses of *por* and *para*

7-18 Tres celebraciones. As you listen to these three brief conversations, write in the chart what the gift will be, for whom, and the reason for the gift.

Conversación	Regalo	Para. . .	Por. . .
1			
2			
3			

MOSAICOS

7-19 Susana Agustín. Listen as Susana Agustín, a third-year Colombian student, tells what she likes and dislikes. Indicate her preferences by putting an **X** in the appropriate column.

	Le gusta(n)	**No le gusta(n)**
los estudios		
la química		
la biología		
conversar con los amigos		
hablar de política		
mirar la televisión		
la música popular		
la música clásica		
la música rock		
bailar		

7-20 En una tienda. Listen to a conversation between Mrs. Rivas and a salesperson. Then choose the best completion to the statements that follow, according to what you hear. You may read the incomplete statements before listening to the conversation.

1. La Sra. Rivas quiere cambiar una. . .
   a) blusa. b) falda. c) chaqueta.
2. Quiere cambiarla porque le queda. . .
   a) grande. b) larga. c) estrecha.
3. La ropa que le muestra la vendedora cuesta. . .
   a) más que la otra. b) menos que la otra. c) más o menos como la otra.
4. La Sra. Rivas necesita la talla. . .
   a) 38. b) 40. c) 42.
5. La Sra. Rivas va a. . .
   a) comprar un vestido. b) probarse una blusa y una falda. c) ir a otra tienda.

Nombre: ______________________ Fecha: ______________________

PRONUNCIACIÓN

Stress and the written accent

The combination of unstressed **u** or **i** with another vowel forms a dipthong which is pronounced as one syllable. **Repitan las siguientes palabras.**

baile fiesta bueno bebiendo sirviendo aficionado

When a written accent is needed because of the rules of accentuation, it is placed over the other vowel, not over the **i** or **u**. **Repitan las siguientes palabras.**

Dios adiós bien también seis dieciséis

As you read the following words, make sure that you pronounce the diphthong as one syllable. You will hear a confirmation after you have read each word.

1. aplaudir
2. emocionado
3. contrario
4. nieve
5. viento
6. escuela
7. guapo
8. canción
9. decisión
10. béisbol

When the **i** or **u** is stressed, the vowels form two syllables, and no diphthong results. A written accent is required over the the **i** or **u**. **Repitan las siguientes palabras.**

cafetería país frío Raúl reírse día

As you read the following words, make sure that you pronounce each vowel separately. You will hear a confirmation after you have read each word.

1. economía
2. geología
3. librería
4. tío
5. reúne
6. baúl

The combinations **iu** and **ui** form diphthongs, with the stress on the second vowel. **Repitan las siguientes palabras.**

ciudad cuidado jesuita veintiuno ruina

Lección 8
Fiestas y tradiciones

A PRIMERA VISTA

8-1 Las fiestas tradicionales. Listen to the following descriptions and circle the holiday that is being described.

1. a) la Nochebuena b) el Día de la Independencia c) el Carnaval
2. a) el Día de las Madres b) la Semana Santa c) la Nochevieja
3. a) la Navidad b) el Año Nuevo c) el Día de los Reyes Magos
4. a) el Día de Acción de Gracias b) la Pascua c) el Día de los Difuntos

8-2 Celebraciones. Identify in the chart who celebrates the holidays you will hear named and describe briefly how each one is celebrated.

MODELO: 0. El Día de los Reyes Magos.

Día	¿Quiénes lo celebran?	¿Cómo lo celebran?
0.	*los niños*	*Reciben muchos regalos.*
1.		
2.		
3.		
4.		
5.		
6.		

8-3 Las fiestas en México. Listen as Ramón and Anita discuss their recent trip to Mexico. Then complete the sentences below based on what you hear.

Anita y Ramón fueron a _______________. Ella visitó la ciudad de Guadalajara y él fue a _______________ con sus _______________. Anita se quedó (*stayed*) con _______________.

Ella tuvo la oportunidad de asistir a una ______________, que es como el rodeo de los ______________. Anita dice que en México un *cowboy* es un ______________. En la fiesta comió muchos platos típicos y escuchó ______________________________________.
Anita, Carmencita y su familia pasaron todo ______________ en la fiesta.

EXPLICACIÓN Y EXPANSIÓN

The imperfect

8-4 Cuando el Sr. Maldonado era pequeño. Listen as Mr. Maldonado describes his life as a young boy. Then indicate whether the statements below are true or false by checking **sí** or **no**.

Before listening to Mr. Maldonado's description, familiarize yourself with the following words:

finca *farm* **ganado** *cattle* **caballos** *horses*

	Sí	*No*
1. El Sr. Maldonado pasaba las vacaciones en una finca.	_____	_____
2. La finca era de sus padres.	_____	_____
3. Su abuelo era muy viejo y no trabajaba.	_____	_____
4. Su abuelo se levantaba temprano.	_____	_____
5. El Sr. Maldonado montaba a caballo cuando era pequeño.	_____	_____
6. Él ayudaba mucho a su abuelo.	_____	_____

8-5 Más sobre el Sr. Maldonado. Listen as Mr. Maldonado continues describing his childhood. Then indicate whether the statements below are true or false by checking **sí** or **no**.

	Sí	*No*
1. El Sr. Maldonado veía muchas películas románticas y de amor.	_____	_____
2. En su imaginación él veía indios y vaqueros.	_____	_____
3. El abuelo no creía las cosas que decía su nieto.	_____	_____
4. Los abuelos fueron a vivir a la ciudad.	_____	_____
5. El Sr. Maldonado compró la finca.	_____	_____
6. Él recuerda con cariño sus años en la finca.	_____	_____

8-6 Cuando yo era pequeño/a. Looking back on your own childhood, say whether or not you used to do the following things.

MODELO: ir a la escuela en autobús
Iba a la escuela en autobús. o *No iba a la escuela en autobús.*

8-7 La rutina del Sr. Montalvo. As you hear what Mr. Montalvo's activities are today, say that he used to do the same things before.

MODELO: El Sr. Montalvo se levanta temprano.
Antes él también se levantaba temprano.

8-8 Alfredo y Mario en Barcelona. Alfredo Vélez and Mario Domínguez spent their junior year at the University of Barcelona in Spain. Tell what they used to do, using the cues you hear.

MODELO: caminar por Las Ramblas
Ellos caminaban por Las Ramblas.

8-9 Cuando éramos estudiantes de secundaria. Answer these questions about your activities with your friends when you were in high school, using the correct imperfect form of each verb.

MODELO: ¿Practicaban ustedes deportes?
Sí, practicábamos deportes. o *No, no practicábamos deportes.*

The preterit and the imperfect

8-10 La historia de la madre del profesor. While discussing the topic of immigration, your sociology instructor uses the example of his own mother. Listen to his description of her experience and then number the sentences below in the order in which the events took place.

1. _______ Celebrábamos la Nochebuena.
2. _______ La madre del profesor se casó en Iowa.
3. _______ Cuando ella llegó a Iowa, hacía mucho frío.
4. _______ Ella llegó a Miami en 1962.
5. _______ La madre del profesor vivió en Miami cuatro meses.
6. _______ Ella fue profesora de español en una escuela secundaria.
7. _______ Los turrones eran el postre de la cena de Nochebuena.
8. _______ La familia celebraba la llegada de Santa Claus el día 25 de diciembre.
9. _______ Los dos hermanos se criaron (*were raised*) en un ambiente multicultural.
10. _______ Los hermanos recibían regalos el Día de los Reyes Magos.

8-11 Las dificultades de Margarita. Listen as Margarita's sister describes why Margarita had difficulties getting to the office on time. Then fill in the chart below, categorizing the events described as completed actions, habitual actions, or background information.

Acción terminada	Acción habitual	Descripción
Ella salió.	*Iba a la oficina.*	*Llovía mucho.*

Nombre: ______________________________ Fecha: ______________________________

Comparisons of inequality

8-12 Cristina y Rodrigo. You will hear statements comparing Cristina and Rodrigo as they appear in the drawings below. For each statement that is true, check **sí**; for each statement that is false, check **no.**

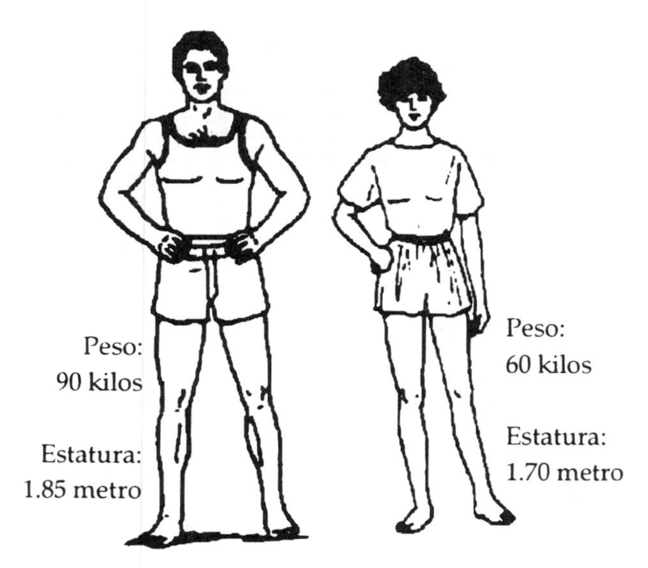

	Sí	*No*
1.	_____	_____
2.	_____	_____
3.	_____	_____
4.	_____	_____
5.	_____	_____
6.	_____	_____

8-13 Comparaciones. You will hear a comparison of two baseball players. Based on what you hear, complete the chart and the sentences that follow it. The description contains some cognates such as **experiencia, ágil,** and **batear** that should be easily understandable.

Jugadores	Edad	Experiencia	Peso *(weight)*

1. Andrés tiene __________ años y Roberto, __________ años. Andrés es __________ que Roberto.
2. Andrés tiene __________ experiencia __________ Roberto.
3. Andrés es __________ ágil __________ Roberto.
4. Roberto pesa __________ __________ Andrés.

8-14 ¿Cómo son? The chart below contains information about two students. Respond in complete sentences to the questions you will hear, using this information to compare the students.

MODELO: ¿Quién es más bajo?
Marcia es más baja que Rafael.

Marcia Mendiola	Rafael Portuondo
20 años	22 años
1,65 m.	1,90 m.
muy inteligente	inteligente
alegre	serio

Nombre: ______________________________ Fecha: ______________________________

Comparisons of equality

8-15 Dos chicos diferentes. Look at the drawing below and listen to the statements comparing the two students shown. For each statement that is true, check **sí**; for each statement that is false, check **no**.

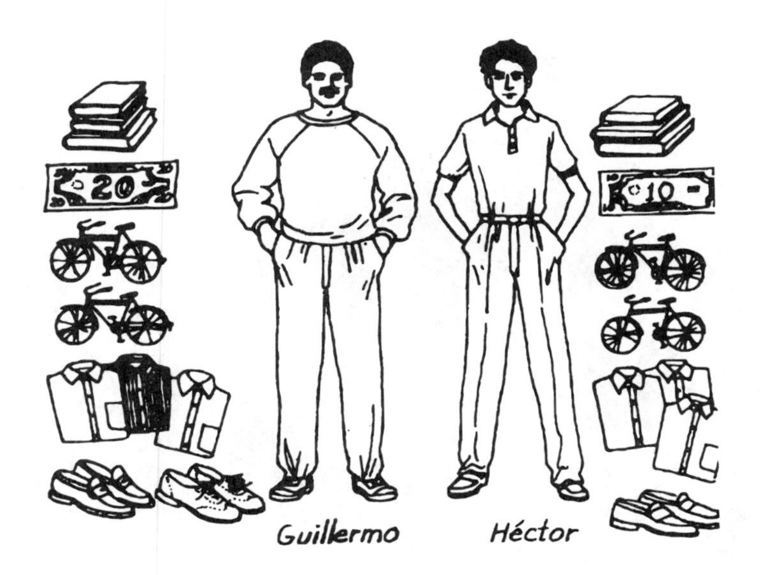

	Sí	*No*
1.	_____	_____
2.	_____	_____
3.	_____	_____
4.	_____	_____
5.	_____	_____
6.	_____	_____
7.	_____	_____
8.	_____	_____

8-16 Más comparaciones. Answer the questions on the tape by comparing the people in the drawing.

MODELO: ¿Quién es tan alto como Arturo?
Carlos es tan alto como Arturo.

8-17 Sus posesiones. Answer the questions on the tape by comparing these people's possessions based on the information in the chart.

MODELO: ¿Quién tiene tantos televisores como el Sr. Mendiola?
La Srta. Valdés tiene tantos televisores como el Sr. Mendiola.

	Sr. Mendiola	**Sra. Sabater**	**Srta. Valdés**
casas	1	2	1
autos	1	2	2
televisores	2	5	2
pesetas	50.000	9.000.000	50.000

Nombre: ______________________ Fecha: ______________________

The superlative

8-18 Una encuesta. As you hear the results of a survey of students' opinions of one another, check off the results in the chart below.

	más				menos
	simpático	**popular**	**guapo**	**listo**	**arrogante**
Víctor					
Aurelio					
Ángel					
Sergio					

8-19 La Semana Santa en Guatemala. Listen as Ana Gutiérrez talks about her trip to Guatemala during Easter Week and describes the famous **alfombras de aserrín** *(sawdust).* Then, complete the sentences below.

1. Las procesiones de Semana santa fueron los espectáculos __________________ .
2. Miles de personas trabajan __________________ para crear las alfombras de aserrín.
3. Las alfombras de aserrín no son cortas, son __________________ .
4. Según los amigos de Ana, la vida de las alfombras es __________________ .

8-20 No estoy de acuerdo. You disagree with your friend's opinions about various people you both know. Correct your friend, using the names provided below.

MODELO: You hear: Juan es el más alto de la clase.
You see: Manuel
You say: *No, Manuel es el más alto de la clase.*

1. Ana 2. Merci y Sara 3. Antonio 4. Esteban y Pepe 5. Josefina

8-21 Importantísimos. Express your agreement with the following statements using the **-ísimo** forms of the adjectives you hear.

MODELO: Robert Redford es guapo.
Sí, es guapísimo.

Mosaicos

8-22 La feria del libro. Listen as Armando explains the Hispanic tradition of book fairs. Then complete the chart based on the information you hear.

Before listening to Armando's description, familiarize yourself with the following words:

editoriales *publishing companies* **puesto, caseta** *stand, booth*

	Feria del Libro	**Día de San Jorge**
Fecha o estación		
Frecuencia		
Lugar		
Participantes		
Cosas que se venden		

8-23 Preguntas personales. Answer the following questions about your age and activities.

Lección 9
El trabajo

A PRIMERA VISTA

9-1 ¿Cuál profesional necesito? As you listen to these descriptions of various situations, circle the name of the professional best prepared to resolve each problem.

1. bombero cajero mecánico
2. piloto arquitecto astronauta
3. plomero peluquero bombero
4. psicóloga obrera recepcionista
5. ingeniero médico secretario
6. abogada ama de casa actriz

9-2 Mi trabajo. You will hear several people talking about their jobs. Identify their professions by writing the corresponding number next to the appropriate profession.

_____ veterinario/a _____ actor/actriz
_____ cajero/a _____ piloto
_____ cocinero/a _____ enfermero/a

9-3 Las profesiones. Listen to the following job descriptions and write the names of the professions that best match them.

1. ________________________________
2. ________________________________
3. ________________________________
4. ________________________________

Explicación y expansión

Se + verb constructions

9-4 Buscando trabajo. Listen to this telephone conversation. Then indicate whether each statement below is true or false by checking **sí** or **no**.

	Sí	*No*
1. En la compañía Salcedo se necesita un director.	_____	_____
2. El anuncio de la compañía está en el periódico.	_____	_____
3. Es necesario tener experiencia.	_____	_____
4. Arturo Castillo tiene experiencia en ventas.	_____	_____
5. Arturo debe hablar con la recepcionista.	_____	_____

9-5 ¿Dónde? Certain activities normally occur in specific places. As you listen to each description of an activity, write its number in the space provided next to the correct place.

_____ banco

_____ caja

_____ biblioteca

_____ cocina

_____ café

_____ estadio

9-6 ¿Qué se necesita? Say that the following things are needed for an important student meeting you are organizing.

MODELO: un micrófono
Se necesita un micrófono.

More on the preterit and the imperfect

9-7 El nuevo jefe. Listen to a conversation between two co–workers, Pedro and Luis. Then fill in the missing words to complete the sentences below.

1. Pedro ________________ al nuevo director ayer.
2. A Pedro le pareció que el nuevo jefe ________________ agradable y que ________________ mucho de negocios.
3. Luis no ________________ ir a la reunión y por eso no lo ________________ .
4. La reunión ________________ muy corta, pero ________________ bien.
5. El jefe de ventas ________________ al Sr. Bermúdez.
6. El Sr. Bermúdez ________________ unas palabras en la reunión.

9-8 Las preguntas después del robo. There has been a robbery at the bank and Mrs. Jiménez, one of the bank officers, is telling the police what various people were doing at the time of the robbery. Match each person with the appropriate action according to the information you hear. Don't worry if you don't understand every word.

_____1. la Sra. Jiménez	a. estaba cambiando un cheque
_____2. la secretaria de la Sra. Jiménez	b. estaba leyendo unos documentos
_____3. la Sra. Iglesias	c. estaba buscando una información en la computadora
_____4. los Sres. Martínez	d. estaba pagando unas cuentas
_____5. Raúl	e. estaban hablando con el Director

9-9 En la oficina. Using the cues you hear, tell what various employees were doing at the office when the director came in.

MODELO: la recepcionista / contestar el teléfono
La recepcionista estaba contestando el teléfono.

Direct and indirect object pronouns

9-10 Los regalos de cumpleaños. Choose the appropriate pronouns from the choices given in the box, and answer these questions about the gifts you received at your birthday party using the cues you hear.

me lo	me los	me la	me las

MODELO: ¿Quién te regaló ese libro? / Marcos
Me lo regaló Marcos.

9-11 Todos los amigos ayudan. You and some other friends have just helped Georgina move into her new home. Using the cues you hear and the appropriate pronouns from the box, answer her questions.

te lo	te los	te la	te las

MODELO: ¿Quién me trajo las plantas? / la familia Sánchez
Te las trajo la familia Sánchez.

9-12 Debes ayudar a los amigos. As the speaker tells you what some of his friends need, tell him you think he should lend them those things. Use the appropriate pronouns from the box in your statements.

se lo	se los	se la	se las

MODELO: Alfredo necesita mi carro.
Se lo debes prestar.

Nombre: ______________________________ Fecha: ______________________________

Formal commands

9-13 Buscando trabajo. A friend is advising you what you should and shouldn't do during an upcoming job interview. If the advice is appropriate check **sí;** if it is not, check **no.**

	Sí	*No*
1.	_____	_____
2.	_____	_____
3.	_____	_____
4.	_____	_____
5.	_____	_____
6.	_____	_____

9-14 En la oficina del Sr. Macía. Your friend Pedro Domínguez is always very impulsive. Listen to his conversation with the manager of a company. Then, indicate whether each statement below is true or false by checking **sí** or **no.**

	Sí	*No*
1. Pedro está en la oficina del gerente.	_____	_____
2. Él solicita la plaza de electricista.	_____	_____
3. El gerente cree que Pedro es el programador de computadoras.	_____	_____
4. Pedro cree que van a despedir al gerente.	_____	_____
5. Pedro va a solicitar el puesto de gerente.	_____	_____

9-15 En un restaurante. You own a small restaurant and are training a young man to assist the waiter and help out in the kitchen. Looking at the list below, tell the new employee what to do.

MODELO: limpiar las mesas
Limpie las mesas.

1. lavar los platos
2. secar los platos
3. poner la mesa
4. servir el agua
5. quitar los platos

9-16 En un almacén. You are in charge of the training program for salespeople at a department store. Look at the list of things a good salesperson does to improve sales and customer relations, and tell the new salespeople to do them.

MODELO: ayudar a los clientes
Ayuden a los clientes.

1. ser amables con los clientes
2. contestar sus preguntas
3. mostrarles la ropa que tenemos
4. buscar las tallas que piden los clientes
5. decirles cómo les queda la ropa

9-17 ¡Muy negativo! Answer your secretary's questions with negative commands and the appropriate pronouns.

MODELO: ¿Cierro la puerta?
No, no la cierre.

9-18 El médico. You are a medical doctor. One of your patients has a bad cold and is asking you all kinds of questions. Answer them affirmatively using pronouns.

MODELO: ¿Puedo tomar aspirinas?
Sí, tómelas.

9-19 En un restaurante. Answer the waiter's questions politely using the cues and double object pronouns.

MODELOS: ¿Le traigo el menú? Sí,. . .
Sí, tráigamelo, por favor.

¿Le traigo la lista de vinos? No, gracias, no. . .
No, gracias, no me la traiga.

Nombre: ______________________ Fecha: ______________________

Mosaicos

9-20 Mis padres. Listen as Lisa, a young woman from California, describes herself, her family, and their preferences. Then complete the chart based on the information you hear.

Persona	Profesión	Le gusta(n)

9-21 Un matrimonio joven. Enriqueta and Pablo are young professionals. Listen to what happened to them last weekend and complete the chart based on what you heard.

	Profesión	Problema	Solución
Enriqueta			
Pablo			

A PRIMERA VISTA

10-1 En el supermercado. Listen as this shopper in a supermarket reads her shopping list. Then look at the drawings below. If the item depicted is on the list, put a check mark in the space provided next to it.

10-2 De compras. You and a friend are having company for dinner tonight. Listen to your friend's ideas. Then indicate whether each statement below is true or false by marking the appropriate response.

	Sí	*No*
1. Su amigo piensa hacer una paella.	_____	_____
2. Ustedes no necesitan comprar pollo.	_____	_____
3. Ustedes van a servir vino blanco.	_____	_____
4. Van a comprar arroz, cebolla y pimientos verdes.	_____	_____
5. Necesitan medio kilo de tomates para la ensalada.	_____	_____
6. Piensan comprar dos manzanas para el postre.	_____	_____

10-3 Una cena especial. Mr. and Mrs. Méndez are having guests for dinner. You will hear a brief description of their preparations for the dinner party. Indicate whether each statement below is true or false by marking the appropriate response. Don't worry if you don't understand every word.

	Sí	*No*
1. Al Sr. Méndez le gusta cocinar.	_____	_____
2. Su esposa no sabe cocinar.	_____	_____
3. Mañana van a tener cuatro invitados para la cena.	_____	_____
4. Ellos no sirven vino en las cenas.	_____	_____
5. El Sr. y la Sra. Méndez van a preparar el arroz con pollo esta noche.	_____	_____

10-4 Identificación. You are helping to set the table for a special dinner. Look at the drawing below and listen to the directions on what to do. For each item you are to place you will hear a number followed by the item's name in Spanish. Find each object mentioned in the drawing and then write its corresponding number in the space provided.

Nombre: ______________________ Fecha: ______________________

Explicación y expansión

The present subjunctive

10-5 Una invitación a cenar. Listen to Petra's conversation with her mother about tonight's dinner party. Then indicate whether the statements below are true or false by checking **sí** or **no.**

	Sí	*No*
1. Los Morales van a cenar en casa de la Sra. Ochoa.	_____	_____
2. La Sra. Ochoa está muy ocupada.	_____	_____
3. La Sra. Ochoa quiere que su hija Petra prepare la cena y limpie la casa.	_____	_____
4. La hija de la Sra. Ochoa va a ir al supermercado.	_____	_____
5. La Sra. Ochoa necesita mantequilla, camarones y otras cosas para la cena.	_____	_____
6. Ella también necesita verduras.	_____	_____

The subjunctive used to express wishes and hope

10-6 Preparando un gazpacho. Antonio Suárez, an exchange student from Spain, wants to prepare gazpacho, a cold soup from the region of Andalucía, for his classmates. Some of them have promised to bring the necessary ingredients. Tell what Antonio wants each person named to bring according to the cues provided.

MODELO: Josefina / pepinos
Quiere que Josefina traiga pepinos.

10-7 La colaboración es importante. Your friends are going to help you with a fund-raising campaign. Tell each person named what you expect them to do according to the cues.

MODELO: Irma / llamar a las personas en la lista
Espero que Irma llame a las personas en la lista.

10-8 Los amigos aconsejan a Juan. Juan Gutiérrez has certain plans for after graduation. Give your opinion of Juan's plans using the cues provided.

MODELO: You hear: Pienso descansar dos semanas.
Es bueno que. . .
You say: *Es bueno que descanses dos semanas.*

The subjunctive with verbs and expressions of doubt

10-9 Marta y Alberto conversan. Listen to this conversation between two friends and to the incomplete statements that follow. Circle the answer that best completes each statement. Don't worry if you don't understand every word.

1. a) un restaurante b) casa de Alberto c) la cafetería de la universidad

2. a) franceses b) hispanoamericanos c) alemanes

3. a) un pescado del Caribe b) un plato mexicano c) un plato colombiano

4. a) no tiene ganas de comer b) no tiene tiempo c) hace mucho calor

10-10 En un restaurante. Ana Celia and Margarita are in a restaurant. Listen to their conversation and to the statements that follow it. Indicate whether each statement is true or false by checking **sí** or **no.**

	Sí	*No*
1.	_____	_____
2.	_____	_____
3.	_____	_____
4.	_____	_____
5.	_____	_____

10-11 Siempre hay dudas. Ignacio is bragging about what he plans to do during a trip he is taking. Express your doubts about each of his claims.

MODELO: Yo conozco al Presidente.
Dudo que conozca al Presidente.

Nombre: ______________________________ Fecha: ______________________________

Informal commands

10-12 Unos buenos consejos. An executive suffering from stress is going to a lake resort for some relaxation. Playing the part of his friend and using **tú** commands, advise him to do these things in order to relax.

MODELO: levantarse temprano
Levántate temprano.

10-13 En la clase de cocina. You are in charge of a cooking class. Tell the people in your class not to do these things.

MODELO: Alicia está sirviendo el agua ahora.
No sirvas el agua ahora.

10-14 Las preguntas de los alumnos. Answer the following questions asked by the students in your cooking class. Use affirmative or negative commands and the cues provided.

MODELOS: ¿Preparo los huevos ahora? / sí
Sí, prepáralos.

¿Saco la mantequilla? /no
No, no la saques.

10-15 La graduación de Miguel. There is a family reunion to celebrate Miguel's graduation and his brother wants to help. Playing the part of one of his parents, answer his questions affirmatively.

MODELOS: ¿Te lavo estas copas?
Sí, lávamelas.

MOSAICOS

10-16 La cena de esta noche. Listen as your friend's mother talks about her neighbors, the Villamar family. Then indicate whether the statements that follow are true or false.

	Sí	*No*
1.	_____	_____
2.	_____	_____
3.	_____	_____
4.	_____	_____

10-17 El cumpleaños de Rosita. Rosita's grandmother is planning a dinner party to celebrate Rosita's birthday. Listen to their conversation and then complete these statements based on what you heard.

1. La abuela de Rosita va a preparar ______________________________.
2. Ella quiere que Rosita ______________________________.
3. Rosita no cree que Pepe y María ______________________________.
4. La abuela cree que Carlos y Ester ______________________________.

A PRIMERA VISTA

11-1 ¿Qué parte del cuerpo les duele? At the doctor' s office you overhear three people describing their ailments. Identify where in the body each person's problem is probably located by circling the appropriate letter.

1. a) la garganta   b) el oído   c) la mano

2. a) el estómago   b) los huesos   c) los ojos

3. a) las cejas   b) la sangre   c) la espalda

11-2 La salud de Isabel. While visiting your friend Héctor's home, you overhear his conversation with Isabel and Susana. Listen to the conversation. Then indicate whether each statement below is true or false by marking the appropriate response. Don't worry if you don't understand every word.

	Sí	*No*
1. Isabel no se siente bien.	_____	_____
2. Isabel no hace ejercicio.	_____	_____
3. Héctor fuma mucho.	_____	_____
4. Héctor cree que su amiga debe comer mejor.	_____	_____
5 Susana piensa que Isabel no necesita tomar vitaminas.	_____	_____

11-3 La buena salud. Indicate whether each of these activities is beneficial to your health or not by checking the appropriate column.

	Bueno	*Malo*
1.	_____	_____
2.	_____	_____
3.	_____	_____

4. _____ _____

5. _____ _____

6. _____ _____

7. _____ _____

8. _____ _____

11-4 Vitaminas. You overhear this conversation at the drugstore. Complete the sentences with the information you hear.

1. La señora está hablando con ______________________________.
2. Ella pide ______________________________.
3. El farmacéutico le recomienda ______________________________.
4. Ella compra ______________________________.

EXPLICACIÓN Y EXPANSIÓN

The subjunctive with expressions of emotion

11-5 ¿Qué le gusta y qué no le gusta a la señora Montalvo? Listen to Mrs. Montalvo's conversation with her teenage daughter and mark the appropriate column according to Mrs. Montalvo's likes and dislikes. Don't worry if there are words you don't understand.

Le gusta	No le gusta	Actividad
		que su hija se ponga la blusa y la falda azul.
		que se ponga el vestido negro.
		que fumen en su casa.
		que su sobrino toque la guitarra.
		que venga toda la familia.

Nombre: ______________________________ Fecha: ______________________________

11-6 Una visita a un amigo. Maribel is visiting a friend who twisted his ankle. Listen to the conversation and then complete the chart with Maribel's reactions in the appropriate column.

Maribel se alegra de que. . .	Maribel siente que. . .

Indirect commands

11-7 Su amiga está enferma. Your friend has a bad case of the flu. Tell what you think is important for her to do according to the cues you hear.

MODELO: ir al médico
Que vaya al médico.

The equivalents of English *let's*

11-8 ¡Vamos a cambiar! In the college cafeteria you overhear this conversation between Aidita and Lucía. Listen to the conversation, then indicate whether the statements below are true or false.

	Sí	*No*
1. Aidita y Lucía van a empezar una dieta.	_____	_____
2. A Lucía le gusta comer bien.	_____	_____
3. Lucía cree que los ejercicios son más importantes.	_____	_____
4. Aidita prefiere los ejercicios.	_____	_____
5. Las chicas tienen opiniones diferentes.	_____	_____

Por and *para*

11-9 Sofía y Dulce van a una charreada. Listen as Sofía and Dulce discuss their plans to go to the **charreada,** the Mexican rodeo. Then indicate whether the statements that follow are true or false by marking the appropriate response. Don't worry if you don't understand every word.

	Sí	*No*
1.	_____	_____
2.	_____	_____
3.	_____	_____
4.	_____	_____
5.	_____	_____

11-10 Un día muy especial para Angélica. Listen to this description of the events surrounding a special occasion involving Angélica. Then complete the statements below based on the information you heard.

1. Angélica quiere comprar un ______________ para su ______________ .
2. Ella va a una tienda con su ______________ .
3. Ellas caminan ______________ la calle Alameda.
4. ______________ Angélica, el vestido azul es el más bonito.
5. Ellas pagan 10.000 ______________ el vestido.
6. Angélica recibe muchos regalos ______________ su cumpleaños.

Nombre: ______________________ Fecha: ______________________

11-11 Regalos para todos. You just won the lottery and have bought presents for some friends. Looking at the drawings, tell who will receive each present.

MODELO: ¿Para quién es el radio?
Es para Susana.

1.

2.

3.

4.

Gilberto

5.

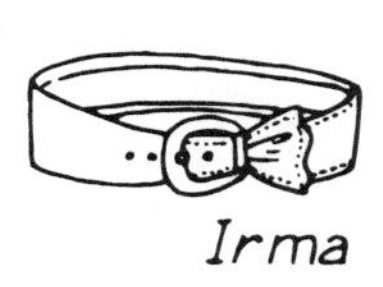

6.

11-12 Opiniones. You will hear the names of several people and their opinions on various topics. Combine both in a sentence using **para.**

MODELO: Alicia / Ésta es la mejor fiesta del año.
Para Alicia, ésta es la mejor fiesta del año.

Relative pronouns

11-13 En un hospital. Listen to these statements about some of the people who work at the hospital where you are visiting a sick friend. Combine the statements you hear with those that appear below using **que.**

MODELO: You see: La secretaria es muy simpática.
You hear: La secretaria está en esa oficina.
You say: *La secretaria que está en esa oficina es muy simpática.*

1. El enfermero es muy competente.
2. El doctor es excelente.
3. El psiquiatra es muy inteligente.
4. La recepcionista es de Chile.
5. El doctor vive cerca de mi casa.

Nombre: ______________________________ Fecha: ___________________________

MOSAICOS

11-14 La enfermedad de mi padre. Listen as a friend tells you about his father's illness. Then listen to the statements that follow and indicate whether each statement is true or false by checking **sí** or **no**.

	Sí	*No*
1.	_____	_____
2.	_____	_____
3.	_____	_____
4.	_____	_____
5.	_____	_____

11-15 En el consultorio de la Dra. Suárez. You have accompanied Mrs. Muñoz to the doctor's office. Listen to her conversation with Dr. Suárez and to the incomplete statements that follow. Circle the letter corresponding to the best completion for each.

1. a) los oídos b) los pulmones c) el estómago
2. a) la rodilla b) el cuello c) la garganta
3. a) unos antibióticos b) unas vitaminas c) unas gárgaras
4. a) tome sopa de pollo b) se ponga una inyección c) beba muchos líquidos
5. a) ir a trabajar b) descansar c) hacerse un análisis

11-16 Dos buenas amigas. As you listen to this story about two friends, complete this chart.

	se levanta	dieta	deportes	le interesa(n)
Marina				
Bárbara				

A PRIMERA VISTA

12-1 Adivinanzas. Listen to these descriptions and identify what mode of transportation is being described by writing the appropriate number in the space provided.

_____ el autobús _____ el auto

_____ el avión _____ la motocicleta

_____ el barco _____ el tren

_____ la bicicleta _____ el camión *(truck)*

12-2 En el aeropuerto. At the airport you hear several departure announcements. Fill in each flight number, destination, and gate number. You will hear each announcement twice. Don't worry if you don't understand every word.

	Número de vuelo	Destino	Puerta de salida
1.			
2.			
3.			
4.			
5.			

12-3 ¿Dónde prefieren pasar las vacaciones? Listen as several students discuss where they would like to go on a vacation combining pleasure with learning. Complete the chart by filling in the place each one hopes to visit, what sports each hopes to participate in while there, and the academic discipline each hopes to learn more about.

	Estudiante	Lugar	Deporte	Asignatura
1.				
2.				
3.				
4.				

12-4 Vacaciones en Pamplona. Listen as a student describes his visit to Pamplona, a city in the region of Navarra in northern Spain. As you listen, indicate with a check mark (✓) what places he visited and with a plus sign (+) which places he and the other tourists in his group liked best. Don't worry if you don't understand every word.

_____ la catedral
_____ el ayuntamiento
_____ la plaza de toros
_____ el café
_____ el Museo de Navarra
_____ el restaurante Arrieta
_____ la Ciudadela
_____ el estadio
_____ los jardines de la Taconera

12-5 Una llamada al Hotel Alameda. Listen to this telephone conversation between an employee of the Alameda Hotel and a client. Then indicate whether each statement below is true or false by marking the appropriate response. Don't worry if you don't understand every word.

	Sí	*No*
1. El señor Castillo reservó una entrada para el teatro.	_____	_____
2. El señor Castillo necesita una habitación sencilla.	_____	_____
3. Él necesita la habitación para un fin de semana.	_____	_____
4. El hotel tiene habitaciones disponibles.	_____	_____
5. El señor Castillo debe llegar al hotel antes de las seis.	_____	_____
6. La habitación cuesta cien pesos.	_____	_____

12-6 En la recepción del hotel. While working on your summer job at a hotel, you overhear this conversation. Complete this summary by filling in the missing words based on what you hear.

Los señores García Urrutia hicieron una ______________________ en el hotel para una habitación ______________________. El empleado no puede encontrarla y el señor García Urrutia va a buscarla en su ______________________, pero el empleado la encuentra bajo el apellido __________________________. Los señores García Urrutia conocen el hotel porque __________________________ allí el año pasado. El señor García Urrutia firma una __________________________ y le da su __________________________ al empleado, quien les dice que su habitación es la __________________________.

12-7 En el mostrador de la aerolínea. Listen to this conversation between a passenger and an airline employee at the ticket counter. Then complete these sentences based on what you hear. You may not understand every word.

1. Estas personas están en __________________________.
2. El pasajero prefiere viajar en la sección __________________________.
3. El pasajero tiene un asiento __________________________.
4. Él lleva __________________________ de equipaje.
5. La puerta de salida es __________________________.

12-8 El viaje de Irma. Irma is planning a trip. Listen to her conversation with Agustín. Then indicate whether each statement below is true or false by checking **sí** or **no.** Don't worry if you don't understand every word.

	Sí	*No*
1. Irma tiene que hacer las maletas esta noche.	_____	_____
2. Ella necesita comprar unos cheques de viajero.	_____	_____
3. Irma trabaja en la estación.	_____	_____
4. Ella va a ir a la estación con su hermano.	_____	_____
5. Irma va a viajar en tren.	_____	_____

12-9 El automóvil. You will hear a series of numbers, each followed by a word identifying a part of a car. Write the number next to the appropriate part of the car illustrated below.

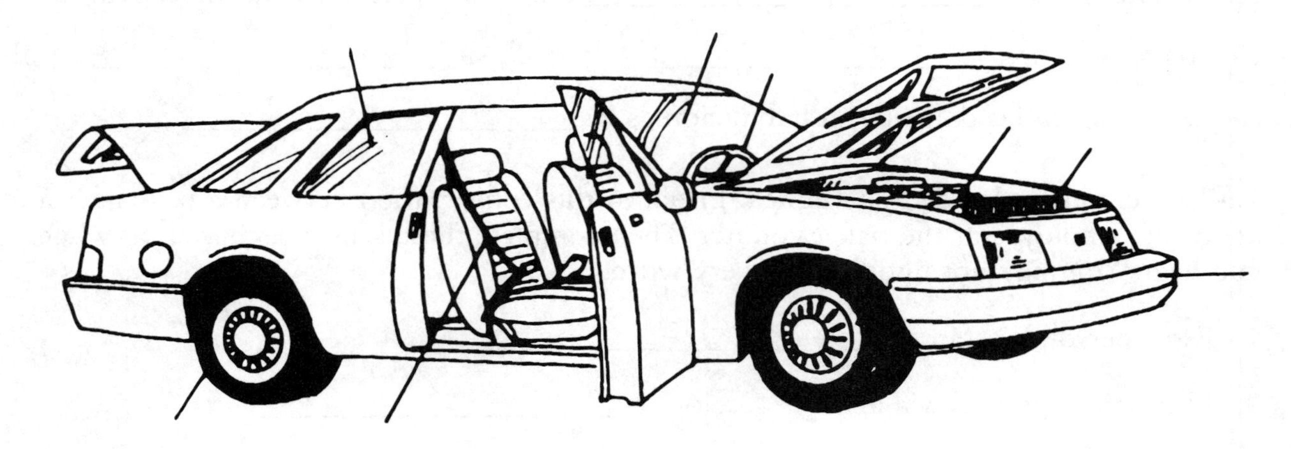

12-10 Un accidente. On the way to class, Arturo meets Juan. Listen to their conversation and to the questions that follow, and circle the appropriate answer to each. Knowing these words may help you better understand the conversation: **vendado** *bandaged;* **muletas** *crutches.*

1. a) Se fracturó un brazo. b) Tiene la cabeza vendada. c) Se torció un tobillo.
2. a) un autobús b) un taxi c) una motocicleta
3. a) al hospital b) a su casa c) a su coche
4. a) en taxi b) en ambulancia c) en tren
5. a) una puerta b) el volante c) el motor

Nombre: ______________________________ Fecha: ______________________________

Explicación y expansión

Indicative and subjunctive in adjective clauses

12-11 Un viaje a Ponce. A travel agent is trying to sell you a travel package for a week in Ponce, Puerto Rico. Listen to his sales pitch and complete these sentences based on the information you hear.

1. El viajero quiere ______________________________
2. El agente le recomienda que ______________________________
3. Ponce está en ______________________________
4. Las atracciones de Ponce que pueden interesarle son ______________________________
5. En Ponce puede comer ______________________________
6. El agente cree que debe visitar la catedral, que ______________________________

12-12 ¿Cómo es Alicia? Tell what Alicia is like, using the information you will hear. Begin each sentence with **Alicia es una persona que. . .**

MODELO: Tiene muchos amigos.
Alicia es una persona que tiene muchos amigos.

12-13 El carro del profesor. Your Spanish instructor is looking for a new car. Use the information you hear to describe the kind of car he is looking for. Begin each sentence with **Busca un carro que. . .**

MODELO: ser barato
Busca un carro que sea barato.

Affirmative and negative expressions

12-14 Medios de transporte. Listen as several people discuss various means of transportation. Then indicate with a check mark what means of transportation they use or would like to use and how often they travel.

Medio de transporte					Frecuencia		
auto	avión	tren	metro	autobús	siempre	nunca	a veces
1.							
2.							
3.							
4.							
5.							

12-15 Un viaje a Quito. Raúl has decided to spend his vacation with relatives in Ecuador. Listen to his conversation with a travel agent and to the questions that follow. Then, circle the best answer to each question among the choices offered below.

1. a) un viaje a Bogotá b) una reservación para el día 15 c) telefonear a su familia en Quito
2. a) que vaya el jueves b) que use la tarifa de excursión c) que viaje en una aerolínea norteamericana
3. a) cuesta menos b) va a pasar más tiempo en Quito c) es su primer día de vacaciones
4. a) no hay ningún vuelo directo b) cuesta más c) el avión está lleno
5. a) hace una escala b) cuesta mucho c) sale muy tarde
6. a) con un cheque b) con tarjeta de crédito c) en efectivo

Nombre: ______________________________ Fecha: ______________________________

12-16 No quiero hacer nada. You don't feel like doing anything today. Answer the following questions using double negatives.

MODELO: ¿Vas a llamar a alguien?
No, no voy a llamar a nadie.

12-17 No estoy de acuerdo. Using double negatives, contradict the following statements about Elías.

MODELO: Elías siempre invita a sus amigos.
No, Elías no invita nunca a sus amigos.

Stressed possessive adjectives

12-18 Un problema serio. Listen to this conversation between Ernesto and Ángel and to the questions that follow. Then circle the letter of the best answer you hear for each question.

1. a. b. c.
2. a. b. c.
3. a. b. c.
4. a. b. c.
5. a. b. c.

12-19 Al llegar al hotel. You and some friends have just arrived at a hotel. Listen to your friends' comments regarding what has happened, and circle the stressed possessive adjective you hear in each statement.

1. nuestro nuestros nuestra nuestras
2. tuyo tuyos tuya tuyas
3. mío míos mía mías
4. suyo suyos suya suyas
5. mío míos mía mías

12-20 ¿Dónde está? Answer your friend's questions about where various objects are, using **sí** and the appropriate possessive pronoun.

MODELO: ¿Tu pasaporte está en el maletín?
Sí, el mío está en el maletín.

The future tense

12-21 En México. You and some friends are in Mexico visiting some Mayan ruins in Yucatán. Listen as the tour guide explains the day's activities. Then indicate whether each statement that follows is true or false by checking **sí** or **no**.

	Sí	*No*
1.	_____	_____
2.	_____	_____
3.	_____	_____
4.	_____	_____
5.	_____	_____

12-22 Algunos cambios. You will hear some sentences describing plans for future changes in an office. Restate each plan using the future tense.

MODELO: Vamos a cambiar los muebles.
Cambiaremos los muebles.

Nombre: ______________________ Fecha: ______________________

MOSAICOS

12-23 Unas vacaciones en el mar. Listen to this conversation between a travel agent and a client, and to the incomplete statements that follow. Circle the letter corresponding to the best completion you hear for each statement.

1. a. b. c.
2. a. b. c.
3. a. b. c.
4. a. b. c.
5. a. b. c.

12-24 Vacaciones en Costa Rica. Elvira and Marcos are planning a one-week vacation in Costa Rica and are asking their friend, Arturo, for some advice. Listen to their conversation and then answer the questions that follow based on what you hear.

1. ____
2. ____
3. ____
4. ____
5. ____
6. ____
7. ____
8. ____

12-25 En la aduana. Listen to this conversation between a Peruvian customs official and an airline passenger at the airport. Then listen to the statements that follow and indicate whether each is true or false by checking **sí** or **no**.

	Sí	*No*
1.	_____	_____
2.	_____	_____
3.	_____	_____
4.	_____	_____
5.	_____	_____

A PRIMERA VISTA

13-1 Líderes de la moda. Many prominent Hispanic fashion designers live in the United States. Listen to this conversation between Eva and Ana and then complete the chart based on what you hear.

Nombre	Nació en...	Vive en...	Premio	Algo especial

13-2 ¿Dónde viven los hispanos? In the cafeteria you overhear this conversation between two students, Jim and Ramón. Listen and then complete the paragraph below based on what you hear.

Jim tiene que escribir un ensayo sobre _______________ en los Estados Unidos para su clase de _______________. Su amigo Ramón le dice que las tres ciudades que tienen una mayor concentración de hispanos son _______________, _______________ y _______________, pero que también hay muchos hispanos en las ciudades de _______________ y _______________. Después le dice que muchos hispanos viven en algunos estados del oeste de los Estados Unidos, como _______________, _______________, _______________ y _______________.

13-3 Los muralistas mexicanos en los Estados Unidos. Listen to an art lecture about the Mexican mural painters in the United States. Then fill in the chart based on what you heard.

Pintores	Años en los Estados Unidos	Ciudades/Estados donde están los murales	Pintores sobre los que influyeron
Orozco			
Siqueiros			
Rivera			

13-4 En la clase de historia. Listen to an exchange between the instructor and a Mexican student in an American history class. Then indicate whether the statements below are true or false by checking **sí** or **no**.

	Sí	*No*
1. El profesor está explicando un conflicto entre México y Estados Unidos.	_____	_____
2. El profesor y el estudiante tienen la misma opinión.	_____	_____
3. El profesor cree que Pancho Villa era un bandido.	_____	_____
4. El estudiante piensa que Villa era un revolucionario.	_____	_____
5. Según el profesor, el general Pershing realizó una expedición a México.	_____	_____

EXPLICACIÓN Y EXPANSIÓN

The past participle and the present perfect

13-5 No hay noticias de Enrique. Listen to the following conversation between Javier and Petra. As they talk, determine whether either of them uses the present perfect or not in their portions of the conversation. Check **sí** if they do and **no** if they don't.

	Sí	*No*
Javier	_____	_____
Petra	_____	_____
Javier	_____	_____
Petra	_____	_____
Javier	_____	_____
Petra	_____	_____

13-6 Las actividades de Silvia. Listen as a friend tells you what Silvia did yesterday. Following his description, the speaker will name several activities. Tell whether Silvia has or hasn't done each activity based on what you heard.

MODELO: lavar los platos
Ha lavado los platos.

Nombre: ______________________________ Fecha: ___________________________

13-7 Las órdenes de la profesora. Your professor asks you and your friend to do some things that both of you have already done. Tell her so, using direct object pronouns in your answers.

MODELO: Abran el libro.
Ya lo hemos abierto.

The past perfect

13-8 Andy García y Guillermo Cabrera Infante. Listen to this account of the friendship between two well-known Hispanics. Then indicate whether each of the statements following the description is true or false by checking **sí** or **no**.

	Sí	*No*
1.	_____	_____
2.	_____	_____
3.	_____	_____
4.	_____	_____
5.	_____	_____
6.	_____	_____

13-9 Mi primer año en la universidad. Tell whether or not you had done each of the following activities by the time you started studying at the university.

MODELO: manejar un carro
Cuando empecé en la universidad yo ya había manejado un carro.
o *Cuando empecé en la universidad yo todavía no había manejado un carro.*

Past participles used as adjectives

13-10 Para identificar. Listen to these descriptions of the pictures below and match the number of each description with the appropriate picture.

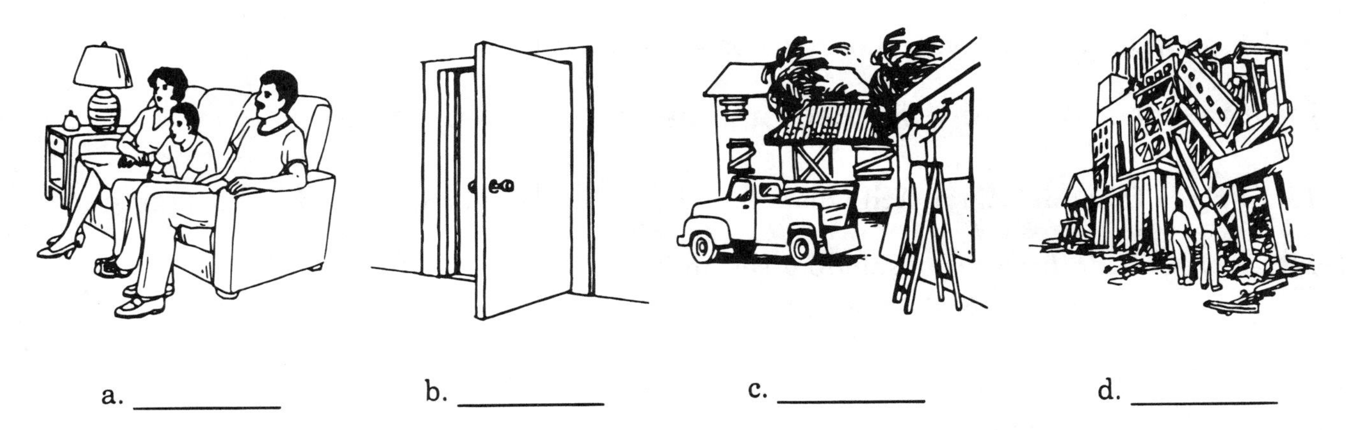

a. __________ b. __________ c. __________ d. __________

13-11 La obra de teatro. You are double-checking what other students are telling you about the preparations for a play your school is putting on. After each report, confirm the information you heard using **estar** and the past participle.

MODELO: Escogieron la ropa de los actores.
¿Entonces la ropa está escogida?

Reciprocal verbs and pronouns

13-12 Un encuentro de dos amigos de la infancia. You will hear six statements describing Javier's activities yesterday. After listening to each statement, determine whether the speaker uses reciprocal verbs and pronouns or not. Check **sí** if he uses them and **no** if he doesn't.

	Sí	*No*
1.	_____	_____
2.	_____	_____
3.	_____	_____
4.	_____	_____
5.	_____	_____
6.	_____	_____

13-13 Una pareja de enamorados. Listen as Gloria talks about Eduardo, how they met, and their relationship. Then complete the following sentences based on what you heard.

1. Eduardo y Gloria ____________________ hace tres años durante unas vacaciones.
2. El primer día Gloria ____________________ un tobillo mientras jugaba voleibol.
3. Eduardo la ayudó y ____________________ al lado de ella para conversar.
4. Durante esas vacaciones ellos ____________________ todos los días.
5. Después de las vacaciones ellos hablaban por teléfono y ____________________.

Infinitive as subject of a sentence and as object of a preposition

13-14 En la fiesta de María. Tell what Irma did at María's party using **al** + the infinitive.

MODELO: Cuando Irma llegó, saludó a sus amigos.
Al llegar, saludó a sus amigos.

Nombre: ______________________ Fecha: ______________________

13-15 Opciones. Circle the letter corresponding to the most appropriate answer to each question you hear.

1. a) Fumar. b) Dormir. c) Caminar.
2. a) Bailar por la noche. b) Practicar mucho. c) Beber cerveza.
3. a) Comer mucho. b) Descansar. c) Hacer ejercicio.
4. a) Hablar alto. b) Hacer gárgaras. c) Cantar.
5. a) Leer con poca luz. b) Beber agua. c) Bañarse.

Mosaicos

13-16 Una máquina de escribir bilingüe. Listen to this conversation between Leticia and Arturo, and to the statements that follow. Indicate whether each statement is true or false by marking **sí** or **no**.

	Sí	*No*
1.	_____	_____
2.	_____	_____
3.	_____	_____
4.	_____	_____
5.	_____	_____
6.	_____	_____

13-17 Un viaje a la capital de los Estados Unidos. Listen to a friend's description of last summer's vacation. Then fill in the blanks based on what you heard.

1. En el viaje a Washington, la familia visitó ________________ , ________________ y ________________________________ .

2. Un aspecto interesante del viaje fue la visita al barrio ____________________ , donde pudieron comprar productos de ____________________ , ____________________ y ________________________ .

3. Más tarde fueron a una tienda de ____________________ que también tenía una gran variedad de casetes, especialmente de artistas latinos como ______________________ y ________________________ .

4. Por la noche fueron a cenar al restaurante _____________________ que sirve comida _____________________ y _____________________ .

5. En estos lugares había ________________ hispanos que se los daban gratis al público.

Lección 14
Cambios de la sociedad

A PRIMERA VISTA

14-1 Diferentes puntos de vista. Listen to the different points of view Elena and her mother hold. Then, complete the chart with a word or phrase indicating these differences in their attitudes and opinions.

Actitudes/Opiniones	Madre	Elena
moderna		
tradicional		
cuidado de los hijos		
tareas domésticas		

14-2 La mujer en la sociedad hispánica. You will hear a brief description of the roles of women in the Hispanic world followed by several statements. Indicate whether each statement is true or false by checking **sí** or **no.**

	Sí	*No*
1.	_____	_____
2.	_____	_____
3.	_____	_____
4.	_____	_____
5.	_____	_____

14-3 El Rey Juan Carlos I. Listen to this conversation between Bob and Felipe, an exchange student from Sevilla. Then answer the questions that follow by choosing the best response from the three choices given for each.

1. a) la historia de España b) el Rey Juan Carlos c) la transición
2. a) en Roma b) en Francia c) en España
3. a) Continuó la dictadura. b) Ocurrieron cambios radicales. c) La sociedad española no quería tener un rey.

4. a) Se legalizaron. b) Se prohibieron. c) Se estableció un partido único.

5. a) México y Colombia b) Francia y Estados Unidos c) ningún país

14-4 Los museos de Madrid. Listen to this conversation between Víctor, who has just returned from Madrid, and his art instructor. Then indicate whether the statements below are true or false by marking **sí** or **no.**

	Sí	*No*
1. Víctor visitó la sala de pintura francesa del Museo del Prado.	_____	_____
2. El profesor cree que el Museo del Prado es muy importante.	_____	_____
3. Víctor habla también de otros dos museos.	_____	_____
4. El profesor ha visitado el nuevo museo del Palacio de Villahermosa.	_____	_____
5. En el Palacio de Villahermosa hay tres pisos con más de 800 obras de arte.	_____	_____
6. Los españoles dicen que Madrid es una gran capital del arte.	_____	_____

EXPLICACIÓN Y EXPANSIÓN

Adverbial conjunctions that always require the subjunctive

14-5 ¿A quién ayuda el padre? Listen to the argument between Luisa and Pablo, and then complete the sentences below based on what you heard.

1. Pablo no va a llegar a tiempo, a menos que ________________________________.
2. El padre va a llevar a Pablo en coche para que ________________________________.
3. Según Luisa, el padre siempre ayuda a Pablo para que ____________________________.
4. Luisa dice que el padre ayuda a Pablo sin que él ____________________________.

Nombre: ______________________________ Fecha: ___________________________

14-6 Una nueva organización contra el uso de las drogas. You will hear incomplete sentences regarding a new organization against drug use. Complete the sentences according to the information below.

MODELO: You hear: El consumo de drogas va a continuar. . .
You see: a menos que / nosotros educar al público
You say: *El consumo de drogas va a continuar a menos que nosotros eduquemos al público.*

1. a. para que/ los jóvenes conocer los peligros de las drogas

   b. antes de que / más jóvenes comenzar a consumir drogas

2. a. a menos que / todos nosotros trabajar juntos

   b. sin que / la comunidad saber cuáles son nuestros objetivos

3. a. con tal de que / nosotros tener una oficina

   b. para que / las escuelas participar en nuestros programas

Adverbial conjunctions: subjunctive or indicative

14-7 ¿Pasado o futuro? You will hear several statements referring to things that have already happened and other things that have not yet happened. Write the number of each statement about something that has already happened in the column labeled **acción realizada.** If the statement concerns something that has not yet happened, write its number in the column labeled **acción pendiente.**

	acción realizada	*acción pendiente*
1.	______________	______________
2.	______________	______________
3.	______________	______________
4.	______________	______________
5.	______________	______________
6.	______________	______________
7.	______________	______________
8.	______________	______________

14-8 ¿Cuándo lo va a hacer? Tell what Augusto Villamil plans to do as soon as certain things happen.

MODELO: You read: Va a ir a España . . .
You hear: tener el dinero
You say: *Va a ir a España cuando tenga el dinero.*

1. Va a pintar la casa. . .
2. Va a comprar un televisor. . .
3. Va a comprarse ropa nueva. . .
4. Va a llamar a su novia. . .
5. Va a pedir más sueldo. . .

The conditional

14-9 Las ideas de Cecilia y Raúl. Listen to Cecilia and Raúl as they discuss what they would do if they had a lot of money. Then indicate whether the statements that follow are part of Cecilia's or Raúl's plans by checking the appropriate column.

	Cecilia	*Raúl*
1. Compraría un coche muy bueno.	_____	_____
2. Tendría una casa grandísima.	_____	_____
3. Viviría en los Estados Unidos y en España.	_____	_____
4. Compraría un apartamento frente a la playa.	_____	_____
5. Viajaría a muchos lugares y países.	_____	_____
6. Ayudaría a los niños pobres.	_____	_____
7. Les pagaría los estudios a algunos alumnos universitarios.	_____	_____

Nombre: ______________________________ Fecha: ______________________________

14-10 Alfredo lo haría. Alfred is always very busy, but you know he would do more things if he had the time. Say that he would do the following things, according to the model.

MODELO: sacar al perro
Sacaría al perro.

The imperfect subjunctive

14-11 En Yucatán. Listen to this description of a visit to some Mayan ruins in Yucatán. Then indicate whether each statement below is true or false by checking **sí** or **no.**

	Sí	*No*
1. Estas personas estuvieron en Yucatán la semana pasada.	_____	_____
2. Los primos les dijeron que visitaran las ruinas mayas.	_____	_____
3. Pasaron tres días en Chichén Itzá y dos en Uxmal.	_____	_____
4. Estuvieron en un hotel en Cancún.	_____	_____
5. A estas personas no les gustó Cancún.	_____	_____
6. Hizo mal tiempo y no pudieron estar en la playa.	_____	_____

14-12 ¿Qué te pidió? Tell what your friend asked you to do by changing the statements you hear to the past.

MODELO: Me pide que salga temprano.
Me pidió que saliera temprano.

14-13 Como si fuera importante. The imperfect subjunctive is also used after **como si**, the equivalent of *as if* in English. You will hear some statements about Felipe, a student who acts as if he were an important person. Change the statements you hear, using **habla como si** and the imperfect subjunctive.

MODELO: Felipe dice que conoce a muchas personas importantes.
Habla como si conociera a muchas personas importantes.

If-clauses

14-14 ¿Qué pasaría? Complete the following sentences by saying what would happen under the conditions given. Use the conditional tense of the verb in the cue you hear.

MODELO: You read: Si tuviéramos tiempo. . .
You hear: Si tuviéramos tiempo /
terminar el proyecto hoy
You say: *Si tuviéramos tiempo, terminaríamos el proyecto hoy.*

1. Si el programa tuviera menos violencia, . . .

2. Si jugaran con los niños, . . .

3. Si llegara temprano, . . .

4. Si comieras menos, . . .

5. Si hicieras tu tarea, . . .

Nombre: ______________________ Fecha: ______________________

Mosaicos

14-15 La mujer en el mundo hispánico. Listen as two feminists, Luisa and Helen, discuss the role of women in the Hispanic world. Then circle the letter that best completes each sentence below based on what you heard.

1. Luisa ha leído un artículo sobre. . .
   a) el feminismo internacional.
   b) la historia de España.
   c) el progreso de la mujer hispánica.
2. Helena cree que las mujeres en el mundo hispánico son. . .
   a) como las norteamericanas.
   b) tradicionales.
   c) militantes.
3. Luisa dice que cuando Colón (*Columbus*) presentó su proyecto. . .
   a) la reina Isabel lo apoyó.
   b) los católicos protestaron.
   c) el Rey pensó que era muy importante.
4. Sor Juana Inés de la Cruz fue una poeta mexicana que. . .
   a) escribió poemas feministas.
   b) defendió a los hombres.
   c) fue miembro de la Comisión de mujeres.
5. La Comisión Interamericana de Mujeres se creó en. . .
   a) México.
   b) La Habana.
   c) los Estados Unidos.
6. Uno de los objetivos de la Comisión Interamericana de Mujeres es que las mujeres. . .
   a) tengan tantos derechos como los hombres.
   b) sigan en sus papeles tradicionales.
   c) hispanas imiten a las norteamericanas.

14-16 La población española. Listen to these comments about the predictions for the Spanish population next century. Then, indicate whether the statements below are true or false by checking **sí** or **no**.

	Sí	*No*
1. Las reuniones se celebraron en la ciudad de Barcelona.	_____	_____
2. Según el investigador Fernández Cordón, hoy en día el promedio de nacimientos es de 1,1 por mujer.	_____	_____
3. En la actualidad, España tiene 20 millones de habitantes.	_____	_____
4. El investigador Fernández Cordón predijo que para el año 2020 España tendría cuatro millones menos de habitantes.	_____	_____
5. Todo el mundo está de acuerdo con las predicciones de Fernández Cordón.	_____	_____
6. Antes las familias que tenían muchos hijos eran muy comunes en España.	_____	_____

A PRIMERA VISTA

15-1 Nuestro planeta. Listen to this conversation. Then indicate whether the statements that follow are part of Gisela's or Ramón's ideas by checking the appropriate column.

	Gisela	*Ramón*
1. Los estudiantes deben hacer algo para mejorar el ambiente.	_____	_____
2. Los estudiantes no tienen el poder para lograr cambios importantes.	_____	_____
3. La Asociación Estudiantil va a colaborar con el proyecto de reciclaje.	_____	_____
4. Es necesario conseguir medios de transporte para que el proyecto tenga éxito.	_____	_____
5. En la cafetería hay muchas cosas se pueden reciclar.	_____	_____
6. Los primeros anuncios van a estar en la cafetería.	_____	_____

15-2 La primera universidad virtual del mundo. Listen to the description of some services provided by the Universitat Oberta de Catalunya in Spain. Then, fill in the blanks based on what you heard.

1. Opciones para los estudios a distancia:

   a) antes: ______________________________ y ______________________________

   b) ahora: ____

2. En el nuevo programa de la Universitat Oberta de Catalunya, los alumnos, desde sus computadoras, pueden:

   a) ____

   b) ____

   c) ____

3. Dos cosas que los alumnos no pueden hacer desde sus computadoras son:

   a) ____

   b) ____

15-3 Los alumnos de la primera universidad virtual del mundo. Listen to the description of the student body for the special program of the Universitat Oberta de Catalunya. Then, complete the chart with the figures based on the information you heard.

Número de solicitudes:	
Número de alumnos aceptados:	
Porcentaje que vive en el área de Barcelona:	
Porcentaje que trabaja:	
Porcentaje entre 25 y 40 años:	
Porcentaje de hombres en Ciencias Empresariales:	
Porcentaje de mujeres en Psicopedagogía:	

EXPLICACIÓN Y EXPANSIÓN

The present perfect subjunctive

15-4 Las instrucciones de la Sra. Martínez. Mrs. Martínez, a physical fitness instructor, couldn't be in class today, but left instructions for her students. Say what she expects her students to have done before their next meeting.

MODELO: el Sr. Pérez / caminar dos kilómetros
Espera que el Sr. Pérez haya caminado dos kilómetros.

1. Ana / correr media hora
2. Felipe / hacer sus ejercicios
3. la Sra. Ferrer / nadar veinte minutos
4. Amalia / subir y bajar los brazos treinta veces
5. sus alumnos / seguir sus instrucciones

Nombre: ______________________________ Fecha: ______________________________

15-5 Ojalá que hayan hecho los preparativos. You are having an important meeting in your office and you hope that everything has been done according to your instructions. Use **ojalá** in your sentences.

MODELO: comprar los refrescos
Ojalá que hayan comprado los refrescos.

1. conseguir una mesa grande
2. traer bastantes vasos
3. escoger sillas cómodas
4. escribir la agenda
5. limpiar bien el salón

The conditional perfect and the pluperfect subjunctive

15-6 El campo y la ciudad. Listen to this brief description and to the statements that follow. Indicate whether each statement is true or false by checking **sí** or **no**.

	Sí	*No*
1.	_____	_____
2.	_____	_____
3.	_____	_____
4.	_____	_____
5.	_____	_____
6.	_____	_____

15-7 ¿Qué habría pasado? Listen to what Gerardo did not do and look at the consequences. Say what would have happened if he had done each thing.

MODELO: You hear: Gerardo no salió.
You see: No fue al cine.
You say: *Si hubiera salido, habría ido al cine.*

1. Gerardo no vio a Luisa.
2. No habló con ella.
3. Luisa no lo invitó a un concierto.
4. No oyó a su cantante favorito.
5. No vio a sus amigos en el concierto.

15-8 ¿Qué habrías hecho? Listen to the following questions and say what you would have done if you could start your life over.

Se for unplanned occurrences

15-9 ¿Planeado o accidental? You will hear about some events in the lives of several people. In some cases the events were planned and in others they were accidental. Write the number of each planned event in the column labeled **planeado** and the number of each unplanned event in the column labeled **accidental.**

	planeado	*accidental*
1.	________	________
2.	________	________
3.	________	________
4.	________	________

15-10 Durante el examen. Listen as a friend tells you what happened to Antonio during a midterm exam. Then tell your friend what happened to you using the cues you hear.

MODELO: Se le olvidaron los verbos./escribir mi nombre
Y a mí se me olvidó escribir mi nombre.

15-11 Mis amigos están preocupados. Some of your friends are worried about the things that have happened to them. Explain why, using the cues given below.

MODELO: Juan está preocupado.
olvidarse el dinero
Juan está preocupado porque se le olvidó el dinero.

1. perder las notas
2. acabarse el trabajo
3. romperse el estéreo
4. apagarse las luces
5. descomponerse la moto

Nombre: ______________________ Fecha: ______________________

The passive voice

15-12 Después del huracán. Listen to these descriptions of the effects of a hurricane. Restate them using the passive voice.

MODELO: El huracán destruyó las casas.
Las casas fueron destruidas por el huracán.

MOSAICOS

15-13 El movimiento ecologista chileno. Listen to the speaker as he talks about ecologists in Chile. You may read the statements below before listening to the selection. After you listen, put an X in the appropriate column to indicate whether each statement is true or false.

	Sí	*No*
1. El movimiento ecologista chileno ha estado muy activo en los últimos años.	_____	_____
2. Algunas personas creían que los ecologistas estaban en contra del capitalismo.	_____	_____
3. Adriana Hoffman es una industrial importante en Chile.	_____	_____
4. Según los ecologistas, en Chile desaparecen muchos bosques todos los días.	_____	_____
5. En la capital de Chile casi no hay contaminación.	_____	_____
6. En la actualidad el movimiento ecologista es importante en Chile.	_____	_____

15-14 La realidad virtual. Listen to this conversation between members of two generations. Then complete the statements based on what you heard.

1. La abuela no entiende lo que es ______________________________ .

2. Su nieto le da un ejemplo usando ________________________ de la abuela cuando ella era pequeña.

3. Héctor dice que el casco que se usa para ver y oír es similar a los que usan ______________________________ .

4. Para tocar objetos, la persona debe ponerse ________________________ .

5. La abuela prefiere leer un buen libro o ________________________ .

6. En algunas universidades, los estudiantes de medicina practican con ______________________________ .

Lección preliminar

Bienvenidos

Las presentaciones

B-1 Formal: 2 Informal: 1, 3

1. mucho gusto / igualmente
2. me llamo Carmen / mucho gusto / encantada
3. encantado / igualmente

Saludos, despedidas, expresiones de cortesía

B-3
1. 6:00 a.m. - 11:30 a.m.
2. 7:00 p.m. - 2:00 a.m.
3. 1:00 p.m. - 7:00 p.m.
4. 1:00 p.m. - 7:00 p.m.
5. 6:00 a.m. - 11:30 a.m.

B-4
1. Usted
2. Tú
3. Tú / usted

B-5
1. Sra. Gómez: regular Sr. Mena: bien
2. Felipe: bien Ana: bien

B-6 4, 2, 3, 1

B-7 1. Hasta mañana. 2. Adiós. 3. Por favor. 4. Gracias. 5. Hasta luego.

Identificación y descripción de personas

B-8 Sí: 2, 4 No: 1, 3

B-9
1. Felipe Torres es activo y competente.
2. Ana Ortiz es moderna y elegante.
3. Martín Gutiérrez es optimista y sentimental.
4. Pepe Chávez es idealista y sincero.
5. Alicia Sarmiento es parcial y rebelde.

B-10 Me llamo Carmen Montes. Yo soy activa y seria. Mi amiga Mónica es diferente. Ella es introvertida y sentimental.

B-11 1. Lima 2. Santiago 3. Madrid 4. Bogotá 5. Caracas 6. Managua

¿Qué hay en el salón de clase?

B-12 1. un pupitre 2. un estudiante 3. una mesa 4. un profesor 5. un reloj 6. un borrador 7. un cuaderno 8. una silla 9. un libro 10. un escritorio 11. una estudiante 12. un lápiz

Los días de la semana y los meses del año

B-20 Respuestas: Hay siete. / Hay veintiocho, veintinueve, treinta o treinta y un días.
Pregunta: ¿Cuántas horas hay en un día?

La hora

B-22 Sí: 2, 4, 5 No: 1, 3

B-23 1. 8:20 2. 10:15 3. 4:00 4. 8:50 5. 7:30

Expresiones útiles en la clase

B-25 A. 2
B. 4
C. 3
D. 1

Lección 1

Los estudiantes y la universidad

A primera vista

1-1 1. a 2. b 3. b 4. b

1-2 Conversación 1: Sí: 2, 3 No: 1
Conversación 2: Sí: 2, 3 No: 1, 4

1-3 Carolina / economía y alemán / difícil / a las once / en el laboratorio

Jim / español / interesante / a las nueve / en la casa

1-4 Por la mañana: Facultad de Humanidades / (answers may vary: escucha, toma apuntes / notas)

Por la tarde: biblioteca / estudia / toma apuntes (notas)

Por la noche: casa / estudia / mira televisión

Explicación y expansión

Subject pronouns

1-6 Tú: 4 Usted: 1 Ustedes: 2, 3

1-7 yo: 4 tú: 1 Ud.: 6 él: 5 ella: 5 nosotros: 3 vosotros: 4 ellos: 2

Present tense of the verb *estar*

1-11 (Answers correspond to illustrations)

cafetería / Facultad de Ciencias / laboratorio

gimnasio / librería / biblioteca

ALGO MÁS: Some regular *-er* and *-ir* verbs

1-13 Sí: 1, 2, 5, 6, 7 No: 3, 4

Mosaicos

1-14 1. Sí: c No: a, b

2. Sí: a, c, d, e No: b

3. Sí: b, c, e No: a, d, f

Lección 2

Los amigos hispanos

A primera vista

2-1 1 / 4 / 3 / 2

2-2 2 / 3, (none), 5 / 4 / 1, (none)

2-3 Ernesto / colombiano (de Colombia) / 19 (años) / moreno (tiene bigote) / en la biblioteca
Ana (Luján) / chilena (de Chile) / 25 (años) / rubia / habladora / en la oficina / en mi (su) casa

2-4 Sí: 1, 3, 5 No: 2, 4

Explicación y expansión

Adjectives

2-5 1. excelente 2. simpáticas 3. bonita 4. jóvenes 5. nervioso 6. contento

2-6 Marcela: alta / morena / ojos negros — inteligente / simpática
Ernesto: bajo / fuerte — (muy) callado
Amelia y Marta: rubias / delgadas / ojos azules — agradables / muy trabajadoras
Arturo y José: morenos / pelo negro / ojos verdes — (muy) habladores / (un poco) tontos

Present tense and some uses of the verb *ser*

2-7 l. a las nueve / 9:00 (de la noche) — en la universidad
2. a las dos / 2:00 (de la tarde) — en la biblioteca
3. a las nueve / 9:00 — en la casa de Julio
4. a las ocho / 8:00 (de la noche) — en el restaurante
5. a las once / 11:00 (de la mañana) — en la Facultad

Ser and *estar* with adjectives

2-8 1. está 2. es 3. son 4. están

Question words

2-10 Preguntas: ¿De dónde es? / ¿Dónde trabaja?
Respuestas: Se llama Carlos (García). / Tiene ojos negros y pelo castaño. / (Llega) a las 9:00 de la mañana.

ALGO MÁS: Expressions with *gustar*

2-11 Le gusta: leer / escuchar música clásica — No le gusta: escribir por las mañanas
Le gustan las novelas: históricas / románticas — No le gustan: las novelas de misterio

Nombre: ______________________ Fecha: ______________________

Mosaicos

2-12 1. a
2. b
3. b

2-13 1. Marta, Paco / tomar algo, hablar / café
2. Inés, Isabel / practicar español / cafetería
3. Sra. Guzmán, Sr. López / trabajar / facultad

Lección 3

Las actividades y los planes

A primera vista

3-1 Sí: 3, 4 No: 1, 2, 5, 6

3-3 Sí: 1, 3, 4, 5 No: 2, 6

3-5 1. pescado / papas
2. jamón / queso
3. lechuga / tomates
4. jugo de naranja / arroz
5. leche / cereal
6. pollo / vegetales
7. café / pan
8. helado / fruta

Explicación y expansión

Present tense of *ir*

3-9 3 / 5 / 4 / 6 / 1 / 2

Numbers 100 to 2,000,000

3-11	1. 287	2. 504	3. 213	4. 704	5. 1.000
3-12	1. 189	2. 293	3. 410	4. 577	5. 886
	6. 764	7. 945	8. 638	9. 1.900	10. 1.000.000

Mosaicos

3-14 Preguntas: ¿Por cuántos días? / ¿Qué van a hacer? / ¿Qué van a comer?

Respuestas: Enfrente de la plaza principal (del Zócalo) / $2.500 / Va a ver películas mexicanas. / Van a beber cerveza (mexicana).

Lección 4

La familia

A primera vista

4-1 (Answers correspond to diagram)

1. Antonio
2. Susana
3. Doña Mercedes
4. Silvina
5. Juan
6. Toño
7. José
8. Julita

4-2 1. dos abuelos 2. veinte primos 3. un padrastro 4. un medio hermano 5. diez tíos 6. tres hermanos 7. siete tías 8. quince primos

4-3 1. padre 2. hermano 3. primo 4. hermano 5. tía 6. madre

4-4 Sí: 1, 5 No: 2, 3, 4

4-5 Ernesto Rodríguez / director de la Biblioteca Nacional / (una persona) ocupada

Rosa Díaz / madre

Pedro / hermano / médico

Cristina / novia de Pedro

Esther / hermana (mayor) / en una oficina

Pablo y Antonio / hermanos / perezosos

Juan Díaz / abuelo / 65 / activo

Nombre: ______________________ Fecha: ______________________

Leonor Roldán / abuela / 65 / tranquila

León (perro) / grande

Explicación y expansión

Present tense of stem-changing verbs *(e>ie, o>ue, e>i)*

4-9 1. b 2. a 3. c 4. c 5. b

Possessive adjectives

4-14 1. mis 2. su 3. nuestra 4. sus 5. mi 6. tus

Present tense of *hacer, poner, salir, traer,* and *oír*

4-16 Sí: 1, 3, 4 No: 2, 5

***Algo más:* *Hace* with expressions of time**

4-18 ocho años cinco años seis meses tres años

Mosaicos

4-19 Sí: 1, 2 No: 3, 4, 5

4-20 el papá: Él quiere ir a la playa.

Pedrito: Quiere nadar y disfrutar de la playa.

Elenita: Quiere (Prefiere) tomar el sol.

la mamá: Quiere (Prefiere) tomar el sol y leer un libro.

los abuelos: Quieren (Prefieren) ver la televisión y descansar en casa.

Lección 5

La casa y los muebles

A primera vista

5-1 Sí: 2, 3, 5 No: 1, 4, 6

5-3 Sala: sofá / butaca / escritorio

Cocina: refrigerador / estufa

Comedor: mesa / sillas

Closet: lavadora / secadora

Cuarto: cama / mesa de noche / televisor / cortinas / alfombra / cuadro

5-4 Amanda: 4 / 5

Felipe: 1 / 2 / 3 / 6

5-5 Sandra: 8:00 / duerme; 9:30 / tiende la cama y limpia su cuarto; 10:30 / mira televisión; 3:00 / limpia la sala y el baño, pasa la aspiradora; 5:30 / corre en la playa; por la noche / va a la casa de unos amigos (a cenar)

Felipe: 8:00 / duerme; 10:30 / lava su auto, escucha la radio; 3:00 / juega tenis; 5:30 / toma algo y conversa (con unos amigos en un café); por la noche / baila en una discoteca

Explicación y expansión

Present progressive

5-7 1. b 2. a 3. c 4. d 5. e

Demonstrative adjectives

5-13 al lado: 2 / 5 cerca: 1 / 4 lejos: 3 / 6

Saber* and *conocer (to know)

5-17 conoce / sabe / sabe / sabe / conoce

ALGO MÁS: More on adjectives

5-19 Conversación 1: 1 / 6

Conversación 2: 5

Conversación 3: 4 / 3

Mosaicos

5-20 Sí: 1, 4, 5 No: 2, 3

Lección 6

El tiempo y los deportes

A primera vista

6-1 1: esquí 2. tenis 3. ciclismo

6-2 Descripción 1: Sí: 2, 4 No: 1, 3

Descripción 2: Sí: 1, 2 No: 3, 4

6-3 Answers may vary.

Explicación y expansión

Preterit tense of regular verbs

6-4 Sí: 1, 6 No: 2, 3, 4, 5

Preterit of *ir* and *ser*

6-7 1940 / fue / vacaciones / amigo / vio / fueron / fueron / fue

Adverbs

6-12 1. a 2. b 3. b 4. a

Mosaicos

6-17 Sí: 1, 4, 6, 7 No: 2, 3, 5

6-18 buen tiempo / quiere / tiene / piensa / estadio / tiene (consiguió) / se viste / llegar

Pronunciación: Stress and the written accent

Dictado. 1. Tú, tu 2. él, el 3. te 4. Tú, té 5. Sí 6. Si

Lección 7

La ropa y las tiendas

A primera vista

7-1 1. b / d 2. c 3. a / c 4. a

7-2 1. camisa / corbata de rayas / traje / calcetines / zapatos negros

2. camiseta / traje de baño / sombrero / sandalias

3. falda / blusa / chaqueta / medias / zapatos

7-4 Sí: 1, 3, 4, 5 No: 2

Explicación y expansión

Indirect object nouns and pronouns

7-5 Rosa / el diccionario

Hermanos de Rosa / el teatro

traje de baño / un almacén

Julia / una bufanda

Gustar and similar verbs

7-9 Sí: 1, 3, 4 No: 2, 5

Pronouns after prepositions

7-12 Con Patricia: Gregorio / la profesora Buendía / Ana

Con Irma: los Gómez / Amanda / Carlos

Some irregular preterits

7-13 1. b 2. a 3. c 4. a 5. b

7-14 1. b 2. b 3. a 4. b

7-15 Sí: 2, 4, 5 No: 1, 3, 6

Algo más: Some uses of *por* and *para*

7-18 1. María Elena / disco / cumpleaños

2. los padres / unas vacaciones / aniversario

3. Diego / traje / bautizo

Mosaicos

7-19 Le gusta(n): los estudios / la biología / conversar con los amigos / hablar de política / la música popular / la música clásica / la música rock / bailar

No le gusta(n): la química / mirar la televisión

7-20 1. a 2. c 3. c 4. b 5. b

Lección 8

Fiestas y tradiciones

A primera vista

8-1 1. a 2. b 3. c 4. a

8-2 (Some answers may vary.) 1. Las familias / se reúnen / comen

2. Los novios (esposos, amigos) / dan regalos / salen a cenar

3. Las personas en los Estados Unidos / hay picnics / hay desfiles
4. Los niños / se disfrazan / piden dulces
5. Los jóvenes y los adultos / bailan / beben champán a las doce
6. Las familias hispanas / se reúnen / comen

8-3 México / Acapulco / padres / la familia de Carmencita / charreada / Estados Unidos / charro / música mexicana / el día

Explicación y expansión

The imperfect

8-4 Sí: 1, 4, 5 No: 2, 3, 6

8-5 Sí: 2, 3, 4, 6 No: 1, 5

The preterit and the imperfect

8-10 7 / 5 / 3 / 1 / 2 / 4 / 8 / 9 / 6 / 10

8-11 Acción terminada: recibió (una llamada) / tuvo que salir / vio / (un auto) se detuvo / la invitó

Acción habitual: usaba (transporte público) / trabajaba (en el mismo edificio)

Descripción: había muchas personas / estaba muy preocupada / estaba en su oficina

Comparisons of inequality

8-12 Sí: 1, 3, 4, 5, 6 No: 2

8-13 Andrés Ortiz / 22 / más / 90
Roberto Fleitas / 16 / menos / 70

1. 22 / 16 / mayor
2. más / que
3. menos / que
4. más que

Comparisons of equality

8-15 Sí: 1, 4, 5, 8 No: 2, 3, 6, 7

The superlative

8-18 El más popular = Víctor
El menos arrogante = Sergio
Los más simpáticos = Víctor y Ángel
El más listo = Aurelio
Los más guapos = Sergio y Ángel

8-19 1. más interesantes 2. muchísimo 3. larguísimas 4. cortísima

Mosaicos

8-22 Feria del libro: primavera / todos los años / en los países hispanos / todos / libros
Día de San Jorge: 23 de abril / todos los años / Cataluña (Barcelona) / los novios (los catalanes) / libros, rosas

Lección 9

El trabajo

A primera vista

9-1 1. mecánico 2. arquitecto 3. peluquero 4. psicóloga 5. médico 6. abogada

9-2 1. cajero / a 2. cocinero / a 3. piloto 4. veterinario / a 5. actor / actriz 6. enfermero / a

9-3 1. astronauta 2. psiquiatra 3. hombre / mujer de negocios / gerente 4. policía

Explicación y expansión

Se + verb constructions

9-4 Sí: 2, 3, 4 No: 1, 5
9-5 6 / 5 / 2 / 4 / 1 / 3

More on the preterit and the imperfect

9-7 1. conoció 2. era, sabía 3. pudo, conoció 4. fue, estuvo 5. conocía 6. dijo

9-8 1. b 2. c 3. d 4. e 5. a

Formal commands

9-13 Sí: 1, 3, 5, 6 No: 2, 4

9-14 Sí: 1, 3, 4, 5 No: 2

Mosaicos

9-20 Madre / abogada y profesora / cocinar platos vegetarianos
Padre / arquitecto / los deportes
Lisa / quiere ser médica / leer

9-21 Enriqueta: abogada / no puso la billetera en la bolsa / pedirle dinero a su médica
Pablo: economista / no puso (tenía) gasolina / esperar para recibir ayuda

Lección 10

La comida y la nutrición

A primera vista

10-1 tomates / lechuga / huevos / limones / carne

10-2 Sí: 2, 3, 4, 5 No: 1, 6

10-3 Sí: 1, 3 No: 2, 4, 5

10-4
1. mantel
2. botella
3. tenedor
4. cuchillo
5. cuchara
6. cucharita
7. vaso
8. servilleta
9. taza con plato

Explicación y expansión

The present subjunctive

10-5 Sí: 1, 2, 4, 5 No: 3, 6

The subjunctive with verbs and expressions of doubt

10-9 1. a 2. b 3. c 4. c

10-10 Sí: 2, 3, 4, 5 No: 1

Mosaicos

10-16 Sí: 1, 2 No: 3, 4

10-17 1. una paella

2. llame a sus amigos

3. puedan venir (ir)

4. son muy alegres

Lección 11

La salud y los médicos

A primera vista

11-1 1. a 2. a 3. c

11-2 Sí: 1, 2, 4 No: 3, 5

11-3 Bueno: 1 / 2 / 5 / 8 Malo: 3 / 4 / 6 / 7

11-4 1. el Dr. Pérez (el farmacéutico)

2. unas vitaminas más fuertes (que las que está tomando)

3. el Forvital 500

4. el Forvital 500 (las vitaminas que le recomienda el farmacéutico)

Explicación y expansión

The subjunctive with expressions of emotion

11-5 Le gusta: que su hija se ponga la blusa y la falda azul / que su sobrino toque la guitarra / que venga toda la familia

No le gusta: que se ponga el vestido negro / que fumen en su casa

11-6 Maribel se alegra de que: Antonio esté mejor / pueda jugar en unos diez días

Maribel siente que: le duela el tobillo a Antonio / no pueda jugar el sábado

The equivalents of English *let's*

11-8 Sí: 3, 5 No: 1, 2, 4

Por and *para*

11-9 Sí: 1, 2 No: 3, 4, 5

11-10 1. vestido nuevo / cumpleaños 2. madre 3. por 4. Para 5. por 6. por

Mosaicos

11-14 Sí: 1, 3, 5 No: 2, 4

11-15 1. a 2. c 3. a 4. c 5. b

11-16 Marina: temprano / saludable / corre dos millas / los deportes / la música popular / el cine

Bárbara: tarde / vegetariana / natación / los libros / la música (clásica) / mirar televisión

Lección 12

Las vacaciones y los viajes

A primera vista

12-1 6 / 3 / 5 / 2 / 4 / 7 / 1 / 8

12-2 1. 120 / Cancún / 10

2. 969 / Madrid / 18A

3. 30 / Santiago / 22

4. 340 / Buenos Aires / 30C

5. 65 / Caracas / 12

12-3 1. Yucatán (México) / natación (nadar) / arqueología

2. San Juan (Puerto Rico) / windsurfing / historia

3. Estados Unidos / correr (campo y pista) / español

4. Pirineos / esquí / arte

12-4 la catedral / un café / el Museo de Navarra (+) / el restaurante Arrieta / la Ciudadela (+) / los jardines de la Taconera (+)

12-5 Sí: 2, 4, 5 No: 1, 3, 6

12-6 reservación / doble / maletín / Urrutia / estuvieron / tarjeta / pasaporte / 612

12-7 1. en el aeropuerto (el mostrador de la aerolínea)

2. de no fumar

3. de ventanilla (en la sección de no fumar)

4. una maleta

5. la 22

12-8 Sí: 2, 4, 5 No: 1, 3

12-9 1. el motor 2. el radiador 3. el volante 4. el parachoques 5. el cinturón de seguridad 6. el parabrisas 7. la ventanilla 8. la llanta

12-10 1. c 2. b 3. a 4. b 5. a

Explicación y expansión

Indicative and subjunctive in adjective clauses

12-11 1. un viaje corto e interesante (que le permita descansar y conocer nuevos lugares)

2. vaya a Ponce

3. en la costa sur de Puerto Rico

4. la playa, los museos, la zona antigua y un ambiente familiar

5. muy bien (platos especiales)

6. está en la parte vieja (de la ciudad)

Affirmative and negative expressions

12-14 1. autobús / siempre

2. avión / nunca

3. auto / siempre

4. tren / a veces

5. metro / siempre

12-15 1. b 2. a 3. a 4. c 5. a 6. b

Stressed possessive adjectives

12-18 1. a 2. b 3. b 4. c 5. b

12-19 1. nuestro 2. tuyas 3. mía 4. suya 5. míos

The future tense

12-21 Sí: 1, 3, 4 No: 2, 5

Mosaicos

12-23 1. b 2. a 3. b 4. a. 5. b

12-24 1. (Piensan ir) para / en Navidades.
2. (Le piden) que les recomiende un hotel.
3. (Es) San José.
4. Porque está en el centro de la ciudad.
5. (Le gustan) los hoteles pequeños.
6. Son amplias / grandes (y confortables).
7. Desean alquilar un coche / auto / carro.
8. (Quiere ver) un volcán.

12-25 Sí: 1, 4, 5 No: 2, 3

Lección 13

Los hispanos en los Estados Unidos

A primera vista

13-1 Oscar de la Renta / Santo Domingo / Nueva York / premio Coty / tiene su propio perfume
Carolina Herrera / Venezuela / Nueva York / premio Moda / diseñó el traje de boda de Caroline Kennedy
Luis Estévez / Cuba / California / Premio a la Excelencia / "la maravilla del año" según *Life*

13-2 Los hispanos / sociología / Nueva York / Los Ángeles / Miami / Washington / Chicago / Tejas (Texas) / Nuevo México / Arizona / California

13-3 Orozco: 1930-34 / Nueva York / New Hampshire / California / Jackson Pollock
Siqueiros: 1932 y 1936 / Los Ángeles / Jackson Pollock y Philip Guston
Rivera: 1933 / Nueva York / Ben Shahn

13-4 Sí: 1, 3, 4, 5 No: 2

Explicación y expansión

The past participle and the present perfect

13-5 Javier: no, sí, no Petra: sí, sí, sí

The past perfect

13-8 Sí: 1, 2, 4, 6 No: 3, 5

Past participles used as adjectives

13-10 a. 2 b. 1 c. 3 d. 4

Reciprocal verbs and pronouns

13-12 Sí: 4, 5 No: 1, 2, 3, 6

13-13 1. se conocieron 2. se torció 3. se sentó 4. se vieron / veían 5. se escribían

Infinitive as subject of a sentence and as object of a preposition

13-15 1. a 2. b 3. c 4. b 5. a

Mosaicos

13-16 Sí: 2, 3, 5 No: 1, 4, 6

13-17 1. la Casa Blanca / el Capitolio / el monumento al presidente Lincoln
2. hispano / Centroamérica / Colombia / España
3. discos / Linda Ronstadt / John Secada / el Puma
4. el Caribe / puertorriqueña / cubana
5. periódicos

Lección 14

Cambios de la sociedad

A primera vista

14-1 Madre (tradicional): no llamar a los chicos / la esposa (mujer) / la esposa (mujer)
Elena (moderna): las chicas llaman a los chicos / los dos / el marido y la mujer

14-2 Sí: 2, 5 No: 1, 3, 4

14-3 1. b 2. a 3. b 4. a 5. b

14-4 Sí: 2, 3, 5, 6 No: 1, 4

Nombre: ______________________ Fecha: ______________________

Explicación y expansión

Adverbial conjunctions that always require the subjunctive

14-5 1. salga ahora

2. pueda repasar antes del examen

3. saque buenas notas

4. se lo pida

Adverbial conjunctions: subjunctive or indicative

14-7 Acción realizada: 1 / 4 / 5 / 8 Acción pendiente: 2 / 3 / 6 / 7

The conditional

14-9 Cecilia: 2 / 3 / 7 Raúl: 1 / 4 / 5 / 6

The imperfect subjunctive

14-11 Sí: 1, 2, 4 No: 3, 5, 6

Mosaicos

14-15 1. c 2. b 3. a 4. a 5. b 6. a

14-16 Sí: 1, 2, 4, 6 No: 3, 5

Lección 15

La ciencia y la tecnología

A primera vista

15-1 Gisela: 1 / 3 / 6

Ramón: 2 / 4 / 5

15-2 1. a) antes: cursos por correo / programas de televisión vía satélite

b) ahora: el campus virtual

2. Answers for a), b) and c) include the following: acceder al Internet / enviar correo electrónico / hacerles preguntas a sus profesores / intercambiar información / participar en debates / ponerse en contacto con otros alumnos / realizar gestiones

3. a) los exámenes

b) reuniones en vivo con los profesores

15-3 1. 2.100
2. 200
3. 50%
4. 90%
5. la tercera parte
6. 63%
7. 77%

Explicación y expansión

The conditional perfect and the pluperfect subjunctive

15-6 Sí: 1, 3, 4, 6 No: 2, 5

***Se* for unplanned occurrences**

15-9 Planeado: 1 / 3 Accidental: 2 / 4

Mosaicos

15-13 Sí: 1, 2, 4, 6 No: 3, 5

15-14 1. la realidad virtual
2. la casa
3. los jugadores de fútbol
4. un guante especial
5. usar su imaginación
6. pacientes virtuales